STEPS
TOWARD
MINISTRY

CONTRIBUTORS

The following individuals have contributed to the content and creation of this equipping manual:

RAY COTTON, Senior Pastor of New Hope Community Church, Portland, Oregon, 1995 to present. Former Pastor of Central Community Church, Wichita, Kansas, 1974-1993.

JEWEL COLLINS, Pastor of Love In Action Ministries at New Hope Community Church.

DAVID DUREY, Pastor of Spiritual Growth, Leadership Development and Marriage Ministries at New Hope Community Church.

DENNIS DEARDORFF, Pastor of Adult Ministries, Pastoral Care and Men's Ministry at New Hope Community Church.

DAN FORD, Pastoral Intern, Assistant to the Pastor of Evangelism, Outreach and Assimilation at New Hope Community Church.

JUDY KENNEDY, Pastor of Women's Ministries at New Hope Community Church.

RIC MARTINEZ, Pastor of Evangelism, Outreach and Assimilation at New Hope Community Church.

JERRY SCHMIDT, Pastor of Business Administration at New Hope Community Church.

BEV SKINNER, Pastor of Compassionate Care at New Hope Community Church.

STEPS TOWARD MINISTRY

One-to-one Mentoring for Effective Ministry

David Durey
Ray Cotton
and others

Foundation of Hope
Portland, Oregon

Steps Toward Ministry: One-to-one Mentoring for Effective Ministry

NOTE TO MENTORS: The authors welcome comments and suggestions for updating and improving this equipping tool. Please submit your ideas in writing to:

FOUNDATION OF HOPE
11731 SE Stevens Road
Portland, OR 97266
888-248-3545
503-659-5683

Steps Toward Ministry: One-to-one Mentoring for Effective Ministry
ISBN: 0-965237-2-6

CONTENTS

FOREWORD

For at least a decade, I have been convinced that the Church is in the midst of the second Reformation. In the first great Reformation, the Bible was, for the first time, put in the hands of the people. And we can be sure that it was always God's intent to put the Gospel message, not just in the hands of the clergy, but in the hands of all the people.

In this second great Reformation, the ministry is being put in the hands of the people. As we look at the historical record, it seems clear that the clergy were never intended to be the primary vessels for doing God's work in the world. In the first two centuries of the Christian Church, there were no clergy. Originally, the faith and the message were entrusted to just twelve Apostles, all lay people. On their deaths, the work of the Lord was left to <u>all</u> His followers.

We might draw some conclusions from the fact that the Roman Catholic Church is presently the fastest growing Christian church in America. They are desperately short of clergy. Meantime, almost all the major Protestant denominations, with a surplus of clergy, are shrinking. It seems to me there is a message there and it is a message that this book emphasizes.

This fresh book is a wonderful resource for the art of mentoring. It also deals with lay ministry, which is essential to this second Reformation. In addition, the book focuses on empowerment not just enlightenment; practice not just theory.

Mentoring comes primarily from Christian leaders who come along-side to model, to encourage and, by example, to teach. It is Jesus' own method. He did not put His first twelve followers in a classroom for three years and teach them theology. They learned as they walked with Him and shared His ministry.

Empowerment is the bottom line of mentoring. "To as many as received Him, to them gave He power to become..." (John 1:12) We may never understand the mysteries of our own nature or that of our loved ones, let alone the mysteries of God. But, the moment we say "yes" to His invitation to follow Him, we can be empowered to be channels of His Spirit.

I believe in the truth and timeliness of this book. I also believe in Ray Cotton and his ministry. New Hope Community Church in Portland, Oregon is practicing what they preach.

Dr. Bruce Larson
Dr. Larson has authored 22 books and served as the co-pastor of the Crystal Cathedral in Garden Grove, California.

INTRODUCTION

OVERALL PURPOSE

The goal of *Steps Toward Ministry* is to provide a format for training and equipping Christians for effective personal ministry and small group leadership.

OBJECTIVES AND BENEFITS

1. Train and equip Christians for effective personal ministry and small group leadership.

2. Obey God's will for equipping and mobilizing the body of Christ for works of service (Romans 12:4-8; Ephesians 4:15; 1 Peter 4:10).

3. Increase an apprentice's competence and confidence. The apprentice doesn't just learn about a ministry activity, the equipper helps the apprentice experience the twelve different ministry activities in an "on-the-job training" approach.

4. Create equippers by empowering those who complete *Steps Toward Ministry* to become equippers of others. Everyone who has been equipped for ministry should take the challenge to become an equipper by reproducing themselves in the life of at least one person each year. The objective is to create "teachers of teachers" and "leaders of leaders."

5. Identify leaders and develop them to their greatest potential. Leadership development is a natural by-product of one-to-one relationships. *Steps Toward Ministry* is a vital part of a leadership development program. This tool provides an opportunity for building a strong mentoring relationship.

HOW TO USE "STEPS TOWARD MINISTRY"

1. **Establish an equipper-apprentice relationship.** An apprentice is one who is seeking to acquire knowledge and skills. The equipper is simply one who has a greater degree of knowledge, experience and skill in ministry. These lessons are designed to be used one-on-one, men with men, women with women. However, they can also be used by an equipper who is meeting with two apprentices or when one married couple meets to equip another.

2. **Explain one-to-one equipping.** Give the *Steps Toward Ministry* book to the ministry apprentice and ask them to complete the Self-Evaluation. Give an overview of the lessons and the tools included in the appendix.

3. **Begin one-to-one equipping.** Allow the apprentice to decide which of the 12 lessons they would like to cover first. Each lesson requires two action steps. First, discuss the ministry skill and the key principles. Second, do the ministry skill together and evaluate the experience.

4. **Keep flexible and center on the needs of the apprentice.** The lessons are designed to be able to be completed in one session. However, take as much time as needed on each lesson to help the apprentice gain competence and confidence. Use the Progress Checklist to monitor which lessons and ministry activities have been completed. If the apprentice has skill and experience in a particular ministry area, the equipper may choose to observe as the apprentice leads someone else through that ministry skill.

YOUR EQUIPPER-APPRENTICE COMMITMENT

We are making a commitment to complete the 12 ministry activities together over the next two to four months.

Equipper:_____Date:_____

Apprentice:_____Date:_____

PROGRESS CHECKLIST

LEADING A SMALL GROUP MEETING Date accomplished: __/__/__
- ❏ Discussed Key Principles
- ❏ Ministry Activity: Plan and lead a small group meeting.

SMALL GROUP DYNAMICS Date accomplished: __/__/__
- ❏ Discussed Key Principles
- ❏ Ministry Activity: Do an "on site" small group evaluation.

SHARING LEADERSHIP IN A SMALL GROUP Date accomplished: __/__/__
- ❏ Discussed Key Principles
- ❏ Ministry Activity: Build a leadership prospect list and share leadership responsibilities among the leadership team and small group members.

A CARE LIST Date accomplished: __/__/__
- ❏ Discussed Key Principles
- ❏ Ministry Activity: Create a Care List.

MINISTRY BY PHONE Date accomplished: __/__/__
- ❏ Discussed Key Principles
- ❏ Ministry Activity: Make ministry phone calls to those on your Care List.

EFFECTIVE LISTENING Date accomplished: __/__/__
- ❏ Discussed Key Principles
- ❏ Ministry Activity: Practice effective listening with someone from your Care List.

PRAYER MINISTRY Date accomplished: __/__/__
- ❑ Discussed Key Principles
- ❑ Ministry Activity: Pray for the needs of those on your Care List and meet with one person from your Care List to pray with them for a specific need.

PROVIDING CARE Date accomplished: __/__/__
- ❑ Discussed Key Principles
- ❑ Ministry Activity: Make a care contact.

HOSPITAL VISITATION Date accomplished: __/__/__
- ❑ Discussed Key Principles
- ❑ Ministry Activity: Visit one or more people in the hospital.

LOVE IN ACTION Date accomplished: __/__/__
- ❑ Discussed Key Principles
- ❑ Ministry Activity: Identify and meet a specific need of someone on your Care List.

INTRODUCING PEOPLE TO JESUS CHRIST Date accomplished: __/__/__
- ❑ Discussed Key Principles
- ❑ Ministry Activity: Practice presenting your personal testimony with your equipper. Then visit someone who needs to know how to become a Christian.

HELPING NEW CHRISTIANS GROW Date accomplished: __/__/__
- ❑ Discussed Key Principles
- ❑ Ministry Activity: Meet with someone who has recently made a commitment for Christ and help them become established and grow in their faith and in fellowship with other Christians.

SELF-EVALUATION

LEADING A SMALL GROUP MEETING

	Low			High	
I have led a small group discussion and feel that the experience was successful.	1	2	3	4	5
I am aware of what to do in preparing for and leading a small group meeting.	1	2	3	4	5
I feel comfortable leading a small group discussion.	1	2	3	4	5

SMALL GROUP DYNAMICS

I have observed and participated in a good small group discussion.	1	2	3	4	5
I know how to establish a good small group atmosphere where everyone participates.	1	2	3	4	5
I have successfully handled people who were causing disruptions or problems in a small group.	1	2	3	4	5

SHARING LEADERSHIP IN A SMALL GROUP

I have been part of a leadership team of a small group.	1	2	3	4	5
I am well aware of the various roles and responsibilities that must be managed for a small group to succeed.	1	2	3	4	5
I feel very comfortable sharing the various roles and responsibilities of leading a small group.	1	2	3	4	5

A Care List

| | Low | | | | High |

I have created a list of friends, family, neighbors and co-workers in whom I have taken a personal and spiritual interest. — 1 2 3 4 5

I feel confident in knowing how to build a list of prospects to invite to a small group. — 1 2 3 4 5

I feel comfortable making a list of people for whom I will pray and seek to serve. — 1 2 3 4 5

Ministry By Phone

I have used the phone to care for others by expressing care and offering encouragement. — 1 2 3 4 5

I feel comfortable with the idea of praying with others on the phone. — 1 2 3 4 5

I am confident that I could make a ministry phone call that was well received. — 1 2 3 4 5

Effective Listening

I have developed effective listening skills. — 1 2 3 4 5

I am comfortable listening to others when they are sharing important personal concerns. — 1 2 3 4 5

I am confident that I know the basic principles of effective listening. — 1 2 3 4 5

PRAYER MINISTRY

Low   High

I have developed the habit of regularly   1   2   3   4   5
praying for the specific needs of others.

I am comfortable praying with people   1   2   3   4   5
personally for their specific needs.

I know the basic principles of intercessory   1   2   3   4   5
prayer.

PROVIDING CARE

I have often taken a personal spiritual interest 1   2   3   4   5
in the lives of those around me.

I feel comfortable responding to the practical   1   2   3   4   5
needs of others.

I know how to encourage and build people up   1   2   3   4   5
spiritually.

HOSPITAL VISITATION

I am confident in what I should say and do   1   2   3   4   5
when visiting the sick and hospitalized.

I have visited someone who was hospitalized   1   2   3   4   5
and feel good about that experience.

I am comfortable visiting friends, family   1   2   3   4   5
and acquaintances when they are hospitalized.

LOVE IN ACTION

	Low				High
I have often gone out of my way to help my unchurched friends and neighbors.	1	2	3	4	5
I am comfortable in serving others through acts of love and deeds of kindness.	1	2	3	4	5
I am confident in knowing how to help those in need.	1	2	3	4	5

INTRODUCING PEOPLE TO JESUS CHRIST

I have taken the initiative to meet with someone to introduce them to Jesus Christ.	1	2	3	4	5
I feel comfortable telling someone how I became a Christian.	1	2	3	4	5
I am confident that I could introduce someone to Jesus Christ if they expressed the desire to know Him as their personal savior.	1	2	3	4	5

HELPING NEW CHRISTIANS GROW

I have discipled a new Christian and helped them become established in their faith.	1	2	3	4	5
I am confident that I know how to help a new Christian grow.	1	2	3	4	5
I would welcome the opportunity to meet with a new Christian to help them learn the basics of following Jesus Christ.	1	2	3	4	5

LEADING A SMALL GROUP MEETING

KEY VERSES: HEBREWS 10:24-25

"Let us not give up meeting together, as some are in the habit of doing, but let us encourage one another — and all the more as you see the Day approaching."

INTRODUCTION

Facilitating a small group meeting can be exciting and fulfilling, especially if the leader follows proven guidelines and principles.

1. Discuss any personal experiences you have had in participating in a small group.

2. Discuss why it is important for friends to gather to study and apply God's Word to their lives within the context and support of a small group.

KEY PRINCIPLES

PLAN FOR THE SMALL GROUP MEETING

(See Appendix A: Small Group Planning Sheet)

1. Determine where the group will meet. Will it be in a home, restaurant, church or elsewhere?

2. Decide the day, time and length of the small group.
    a. Will the group meeting last one hour or will it be longer?
    b. Will the group meet for a few weeks, months or be on-going?

3. Choose the type of people to target.
    a. Will the group be for men, women or both?

b.   What ages will be represented in the group?

c.   Will the group be for singles, married couples or both?

d.   Will it be a neighborhood or workplace group?

4.   Select study materials for the group.
a.   What topic(s) or Bible passage(s) will be used?
b.   Will a published study guide be used?
c.   Make sure your study materials fit your "type" of group.

5.   Recruit help by building a leadership team for the group (see the lesson, Sharing Leadership In A Small Group).

6.   Create a prospect list of those you wish to attend the group (see the lesson, A Care List). Use your personal circle of relationships to build the group: family, neighbors, friends at work, church, school, clubs or other organizations in which you participate.

PREPARE FOR THE SMALL GROUP MEETING

1.   Arrive 20 minutes before the meeting to pray with the leadership team.

2.   Make the location of the meeting conducive to good group dynamics.
a.   Try to maintain a setting that is free of interruptions.
b.   Create an uplifting setting with good lighting.
c.   Engage the help of the host to maintain an atmosphere of love, warmth and acceptance.
d.   Arrange seating in a circle and have extra chairs available.
e.   Provide for drinks and refreshments.
f.   Have copies of the discussion guide ready to distribute.
g.   Have extra Bibles and pens available.

3.   Greet arriving guests with warmth and hospitality. You may choose to offer food and refreshments prior to, during or after the meeting.

PRESENT A BALANCED SMALL GROUP MEETING[1]

Make it a priority to balance the three necessary elements for an effective meeting: Shared Life (15 minutes) Conversational Prayer

(15 minutes) and Bible Application (30 minutes). (See Appendix B: Small Group Meeting Checklist)

1. **Shared Life.** The first 15 minutes of the meeting are usually reserved for the sharing of life. This allows friendships to develop and deepen as members get better acquainted and find common points of interest or need. This sharing time may include several of the following components:
   a. Welcome and opening prayer.
   b. Introduction of guests.
   c. Fun ice breaker activities or questions.
   d. Testimonies or reports of answered prayer.
   e. Expressions of appreciation for one another.
   f. Worship through singing.
   g. Announcements.

2. **Conversational Prayer.** The next 5-10 minutes are devoted to conversational prayer. Conversational prayer is a very effective way to pray in a small group. It is a prayer which unites people in conversation with God and with each other.
   a. This simply means talking to God in an easy, natural conversation.
   b. Each person should feel free to pray several times using short sentence prayers.
   c. No one person should dominate the prayer time.
   d. Several people should pray short sentences on each topic before changing to a new prayer focus.
   e. No one should ever feel forced to pray out loud.
   f. It is best not to go around the circle and take prayer requests but to have people state out their requests as the group is praying conversationally.
   g. Conversational prayer is topical prayer. Prayer starters can include thanking God for what He has done; asking God to do something for a person within the group; praising God for who He is, etc.

3. **Bible Application (30 minutes).** The goal of a small group is to apply the Bible to everyday life, learning to live in obedience to God.
   a. Start with an opener question. The discussion guide should begin with an opener question which will point the

conversation in the direction of the topic. Example: "How do you explain why bad things happen to nice people?"

b.   Read the Bible passage and discuss the lesson. The discussion guide should have six to eight questions that help the group explore the lesson.

1)   Some questions should have answers that only the Bible can provide. Example: What made Paul confident that God would take care of His people? (Romans 8:31-32)

2)   Some questions should be "thought" questions which allow anyone to offer an opinion or perspective. Example: What gives Christians confidence to face difficult times?

c.   Apply the Bible lesson to everyday life. The discussion guide should have a closing application question which helps group members think about how they can use the Bible lesson in their lives this week. Example: What can you do this week to demonstrate that you are trusting God to work out your circumstances for good?

4.   **Close with Conversational Prayer (five minutes).** The primary focus of this closing prayer is the application of Bible truths in the lives of group members. "Lord, help me this week to apply to my life what you have shown me in your Word today."

MINISTRY ACTIVITY:
With the support and help of your equipper, plan and lead a small group meeting (see Appendix B: Small Group Meeting Checklist).

1.   Time:

2.   Date:

3.   Complete the Small Group Meeting Checklist.

REFLECTION AND EVALUATION

1.   What things went well?

2.   What did you enjoy most about this ministry activity?

3.   What would you do differently next time?

SMALL GROUP DYNAMICS

KEY VERSE: 1 THESSALONIANS 5:11

"Therefore encourage one another and build each other up, just as in fact you are doing."

INTRODUCTION

What are the elements that create an exciting small group meeting? Why is it that some groups seem full of life while others, studying the same material, seem dry and dull? There are principles of group dynamics that can make or break a small group meeting.

1. Discuss together any personal experiences you have had in leading a small group meeting or Bible study.

2. Discuss what you enjoy about small groups and what benefits you have observed.

KEY PRINCIPLES

ESTABLISH AN ATMOSPHERE OF LOVE[1]

1. Practice mutual edification (Romans 14:19).
   a. Seek to build each other up. Affirm one another. We want to build healthy self-esteem in each member.
   b. Pastoral care is a natural by-product of small groups. The leader, assistant and host need to set the example in how they express love and care for each other.

2. Encourage everyone in the group.
    a. Make each person feel important. Let them know that their ideas and comments are valued.
    b. Avoid focusing advise on just one member of the group. This is not a counseling session.

3. Respond lovingly to a need expressed. . .immediately.
    a. Pray immediately when a need is expressed. Don't make a list of prayer requests before you start praying, pray when the first need is expressed.
    b. Teach by example. When you as the leader have a need, share it and ask the group to pray for you.
    c. The "Love Seat." A chair can be placed in the middle of the circle while people gather around and gently lay their hands on the person in the "love seat" and pray for their need.

SEEK TO GAIN EVERYONE'S PARTICIPATION

1. The leader is a facilitator not the authority or teacher.
    a. "Play Dumb." The leader should not respond to every question. You must allow the group members to give their input.
    b. Don't be afraid of silence. Sometimes the leader must be quiet and wait for the members to formulate their response to a question.
    c. "Cave Exploring." The Bible is the "cave." Don't stand at the entrance of the cave telling the group what you've seen inside, take them in and let them explore for themselves.

2. How you arrange the seating makes a difference.
    a. Sit in a Circle. Arranging the seating in a circle allows everyone to feel included.
    b. Same Eye Level. It is best if the members of the group can sit at the same eye level.
    c. Only One Extra Chair. Avoid having several empty chairs. A feeling of closeness is lost if the groups members are seated too far apart. Add chairs as they are needed.
    d. Eye Contact. Make sure that everyone can see each of the members of the group.

3. Everyone is encouraged to participate but no one is required to
    pray, read or speak.
    a. Don't Hog – Don't Hide. Everyone is encouraged to share
        but no one is allowed to dominate.
    b. Don't Go Around the Circle. Avoid a pattern of reading,
        praying or sharing around the circle. This causes people to
        feel obligated to participate.

HANDLE PROBLEM PEOPLE IN A POSITIVE WAY[2]

1. Handle problem people away from the group on a one-to-one
    basis.
    a. "No dumping permitted." A disturbed person cannot
        become the center of attention. Make it clear that everyone
        is loved but that "no dumping is permitted."
    b. Refer troubled people to support groups. A disturbed person
        may need to be asked to join a support group which can
        better address their needs.

2. Don't allow people to confess anyone else's faults but their own.
    a. No Gossip. Don't talk about people outside the group.
    b. Focus on helping those in the group by asking "How can we
        pray for you?"

3. Don't allow doctrinal discussion that is divisive or argumentative.
    Simply say, "I'll be happy to discuss this with you after the meet-
    ing," or, "I'll go with you to ask our pastor about that doctrinal
    issue if it is important to you."

4. Don't allow anyone to do all the talking.
    a. Don't give frequent eye contact to the talker.
    b. Have the talker sit next you, not across from you.
    c. Have your assistant help you keep on track without you
        having to directly confront the talker. Have them say,
        "Thank you for your comments. Now let's hear from some
        one else," or, "Let's continue our lesson with the next
        question."
    d. If the situation persists, confront the "talker" one-on-one
        away from the group. Tell them that they must stop

dominating the discussions and explain that everyone needs
an opportunity to contribute.

MINISTRY ACTIVITY: DO AN "ON SITE" SMALL GROUP EVALUATION

Visit a small group and observe how the leaders functioned in compar-
ison to the principles listed above. Complete the worksheet in
Appendix C: Good Group Dynamics. After visiting the small group,
meet alone with your equipper and compare your insights.

1.   Time:

2.   Date:

3.   Leaders and hosts of group that you visited:

REFLECTION AND EVALUATION

1.   What things went well?

2.   What did you enjoy most about the small group meeting?

3.   What would you have done differently?

SHARING LEADERSHIP IN A SMALL GROUP

KEY VERSE: 1 PETER 4:10

"Each one should use whatever gift he has received to server others, faithfully administering God's grace in its various forms."

INTRODUCTION

It has been said, "many hands make light work." This statement is also true for sustaining a successful small group.

1. Discuss any personal experiences you have had in observing a small group. Did the leader do it all? Did you assist in any way? What leadership roles did the group have?

2. Discuss why it is important to have a team of people leading a small group, rather than one person who does it all.

KEY PRINCIPLES

THE NEED TO SHARE LEADERSHIP IN A SMALL GROUP

1. List the leadership responsibilities. To illustrate the need to share the leadership load of a small group, make a list of all the responsibilities that must be taken care of for a group to succeed. The following items will serve as a start:
    a. Lesson selection and preparation.
    b. Facilitate Bible lesson discussion.
    c. Lead group in conversational prayer.
    d. Lead group in sharing about their week.
    e. Meeting place set-up and preparation.

    f.   Greeting guests as they arrive.
    g.   Refreshments coordinated.
    h.   Child care.
    i.   Handling phone calls and interruptions.
    j.   Phone calls to group between meetings.
    k.   Invitations to new people.
    l.   Visits to meet the needs of group members.
    m. Other leadership responsibilities. . .

2.   Share the leadership responsibilities. Here is a simple formula for successful small group leadership:
    a.   One leader doing it all = burnout and end of the small group.
    b.   Two people sharing leadership = maintaining the small group.
    c.   Three people sharing leadership = multiplication of small groups.

THE SMALL GROUP LEADERSHIP TEAM[1]

There are three vital small group leadership positions: the leader, the assistant leader and the host. When each person functions in their role, it encourages the others, lightens the load and makes the group successful.

1.   The Leader: This person or couple is ultimately responsible for the small group. They ensure what is necessary to fulfill its purpose.

2.   The Assistant Leader: This person may be co-leading with years of experience in small group leadership or they may be just beginning as an apprentice leader. Either way, they are free to assist in any aspects of small group leadership and responsibility as they work with the leadership team.

3.   The Host: This person or couple is responsible for providing the location, set-up, refreshments and positive atmosphere for the small group meeting. They also assist in greeting attendees.

FOUR GOALS OF THE LEADERSHIP TEAM

1.   Discipleship: The leadership team is concerned that everyone

in the group is growing in spiritual maturity through fellowship and application of God's Word.

2. Care: The leadership team must answer these questions:
   a. Are we aware of the needs of the group members?
   b. Are the group members involved in meeting each other's needs?
   c. Are the needs of the group being met adequately?

3. Service: The leadership team continually looks for opportunities to express the love of Jesus by meeting the tangible needs of group members and those in the community.

4. Outreach: The leadership team must continue to motivate group members to bring unchurched people into the group.

BUILDING A LEADERSHIP TEAM

1. Build a leadership prospect list. Look for people with the following qualities:
   a. People with a heart and vision for ministry.
   b. People who demonstrate loyalty and teamwork.
   c. People who have positive influence on others in group settings.
   d. People who are F.A.T.:
      1) Faithful to God and others.
      2) Available for ministry assignments.
      3) Teachable. Willing to learn.

2. Prayerfully evaluate your prospects. Look for these characteristics:[2]
   a. Enthusiasm: A positive outlook and a love for God and people.
   b. Clear testimony: A clear Christian testimony of what God has done and is doing in their life.
   c. Dedication: A clear commitment to the success of the group.
   d. Spirit-directed life: A life submitted to the control and empowerment of the Holy Spirit.
   e. Time and means: The prospect must have adequate time available to give to leading and developing the small group.

3. Invite your leadership prospects into service:
    a. Ask your prospect to help lead different parts of the group meeting.
    b. Give your prospect additional opportunities to serve as they prove responsive and faithful.
    c. Employ "Planned Absence." When you know that you can not attend the small group meeting, ask your leadership prospect to take your place in facilitating the meeting.
    d. Affirm your prospect when they succeed in a ministry task.
    e. Invite your prospect to become part of the leadership team of the small group.
    f. Continue offering counsel and feedback on their performance.

MINISTRY ACTIVITY: SHARE THE LEADERSHIP OF A SMALL GROUP
Meet with your equipper to do the following:

1. Take inventory of your small group leadership team.

    Leader: _____

    Assistant: _____

    Host: _____

2. List the responsibilities that need to be covered for your group.
3. Build a leadership prospect list. Who do you want to invite into service?
4. Divide the responsibilities among your leadership team and group.

REFLECTION AND EVALUATION

1. What things are going well for your small group leadership?

2. What excites you the most about sharing leadership in a small group?

3. What changes need to be made at this time?

A CARE LIST

KEY VERSES: GALATIANS 6:9-10

"Let us not become weary in doing good, for at the proper time we will reap a harvest if we do not give up. Therefore, as we have opportunity, let us do good to all people, especially to those who belong to the family of believers."

INTRODUCTION

God has given to each of us a sphere of influence where we can effectively minister to others. Creating a Care List helps us recognize who those people are and to be aware of the opportunities God gives us to show them love and concern.

1. Discuss any personal experience you have had in using a Care List.

2. Discuss why it is important and helpful to keep a list of those for whom you take a spiritual interest.

KEY PRINCIPLES

CREATING YOUR CARE LIST

1. What is a Care List?
    a. A Care List simply identifies the people for whom you have taken a spiritual interest.
    b. It is a key tool for building an effective personal ministry to others.
    c. It becomes a "personal action list" that gives specific focus regarding your desire to have God use you.
    d. It could be called a "Ministry Opportunity List."

2. Who should be on your Care List?
    a. People who attend your small group.
    b. Prospects for your small group.
    c. Those in your circle of influence: friends, family, neighbors and co-workers in whom you have a spiritual interest.
    d. People referred to you by your church.

3. How do you build your Care List?
    a. **Pray for God's guidance.** Ask God who you should include. God will often lead you by giving you a burden for or a special interest in certain people.
    b. **Create your Care List** from within your area of ministry and spheres of influence:
        1) List all those who are active, inactive or prospective members of your small group.
        2) Include close personal relationships within your circle of influence: family, neighbors, friends at work, church, school, clubs, or other organizations in which you participate.
        3) Identify people that have been drawn to you or that have looked to you for guidance.
    c. **Organize your Care List** in a ministry contact record notebook. (See Appendix D: Ministry Contact Records.)
        1) Create an alphabetical directory of your Care List, including the name, phone number and address of each person.
        2) Include a birth date and anniversary date if applicable.
        3) Include the names of immediate family members. Remember, these are the most important people in this person's life and often one of them will answer the phone when you call.
        4) Maintain a ministry contact journal for each person on your list where you can record the dates and brief information about your contacts.

4. How do you build a "small group prospect list"? Joining a small group is one of the most effective ways to help people grow spiritually and personally. It is important to help those on your Care List find their way into a small group. However, not everyone on your Care List should be in your particular small group. You must develop a unique prospect list that fits your small group.

a. Choose the type of people to target.
   1) Will the group be for men, women, or both?
   2) What ages will be represented in the group?
   3) Will the group be for singles, married couples or both?
   4) Will it be a neighborhood or workplace group?
b. Build your small group prospect list.
   1) Generally speaking, there is a 3:1 ratio between the total number you are inviting and the average attendance of your group. If you want a group attendance of 10 people, you need to have 30 people on your small group prospect list.
   2) Include the appropriate people from your personal circle of influence on this list.
   3) Have your small group leadership team add to this list.
   4) Ask your pastor or church leaders for names and referrals for your small group prospect list.

CULTIVATING YOUR CARE LIST

1. **Pray for your Care List.** Take a spiritual interest in these people and pray for them regularly.
   a. Pray that God will work in the lives of each person on your list even if they can't or don't come to your small group or church.
   b. Find out specific needs and note them in your prayer journal so you can pray in a personal way for them.
   c. Pray that God will give you specific opportunities to show love and concern for these people.
   d. Pray that those who have not accepted Christ will come to a personal relationship with Him.

2. **Contact your Care List.** Make regular contact with each person on your Care List.
   a. Contact each person on your small group prospect list and invite them to participate in the group.
   b. Realize that you may need to make several additional contacts with those on your small group prospect list in order to gain their participation.
   c. Keep in regular contact with those on your small group list between group meetings, especially when a person has been

        unable to attend that week.
- d.   Record your contact in your Ministry Contact Records journal.

3. **Respond to life events and personal needs.** Make the most of natural opportunities.
   - a.   Use special life events such as birthdays, anniversaries, births, etc., to send a special card or note.
   - b.   Find out specific needs in the person's life and respond with positive caring behavior where appropriate.
   - c.   Give words of encouragement and appreciation. A note or short phone call can mean a lot.
   - d.   Be respectful of the person's time and lifestyle when making your contacts.
   - e.   Respond to crisis in the person's life with loving concern (see lesson, Providing Care).

MINISTRY ACTIVITY: CREATE A CARE LIST Follow the steps listed

above for creating a Care List. Use the Care List worksheets on pages 73-76 in Appendix D.

1. Time:
2. Date:
3. Number of small group members?
   Number on your small group prospect list?
   Number on your circle of influence list?

REFLECTION AND EVALUATION

1. How easy or difficult was it for you to create your Care List?

2. What did you enjoy most about this ministry activity?

3. What do you need to do to keep your list current and use it effectively?

MINISTRY BY PHONE

KEY VERSES: ROMANS 12:10, 15

"Be devoted to one another in brotherly love. . . . Honor one another above yourselves. Rejoice with those who rejoice; mourn with those who mourn."

INTRODUCTION

The phone has become an important part of our daily lives. The phone can also become a very useful tool for personal ministry. Many people welcome a phone call who would not receive a personal visit.

1. Discuss any personal experiences you have had when someone called you to encourage you and pray with you.

2. Discuss how a ministry phone call can be as helpful and even more well received than a personal visit.

KEY PRINCIPLES

THE KEYS TO SUCCESSFUL MINISTRY BY PHONE

1. Prepare your heart by praying. Ask God to give you the words to speak. Trust God to work through you and give you complete peace.

2. Before you call, make sure that you know how you will pronounce their name and what you are going to say.

3. When they answer the phone, introduce yourself, your ministry role (small group leader, etc.), and tell them the name of your church.

4. Immediately ask them if they have a moment to talk. Offer to call at another time if they are busy.

5. Get a feel for how the person is doing at the time of your call. Ask them how their day or evening is going. Even though most say "fine," you can usually sense their attitude by their tone of voice.

6. State the purpose of your call: To thank them for attending your church, to invite them to your small group, to follow-up on a spiritual commitment or to follow-up on a prayer request (see Sample Ministry Phone Calls Appendix D: Ministry Contact Records).

7. Affirm that you care about them. Ask if they have any prayer requests. If they share a prayer request, listen carefully and write it down on a Ministry Contact Records journal sheet.

8. Ask if you may pray with them about it right now. If they allow you to, pray a short prayer with them about their concern. At the close of your prayer, thank them for sharing, then end the conversation.[1]

9. If they do not want to pray with you for their request, tell them that you will pray for them as soon as you hang up. Thank them for sharing their request, end the conversation, then pray for the need before doing anything else.

10. Keep a record of the prayer request on a Ministry Contact Records journal sheet so that you can ask about it the next time you call.

SOME "DON'TS" IN MINISTRY BY PHONE

1. Don't ask any questions before you identify yourself.

2. Don't try to keep someone on the phone if they are busy.

3. Don't discuss any aspect of your conversation with others; this can be gossip, and it can ruin your credibility.

SOME THINGS "TO DO" IN MINISTRY BY PHONE

1. Make sure the other person is your first concern. Be willing to listen. People need a sympathetic ear.

2. Be friendly, kind and compassionate. Remember, a smile can be "heard" over the phone.

3. Keep the phone call short. You do not want to be a burden and you want them to look forward to your next call.

4. PRAY! Ask God to give you the words to say.

SAMPLE MINISTRY PHONE CALL

1. Greeting:
   *Hello, my name is _____ and
   I'm a _____(small group leader, etc.) At
   Church. Is_____ there, please? Thank you.*

2. Permission:
   *Is this a convenient time to talk? (If yes, continue; if no, offer to
   call again)*

3. Perspective:
   How are you doing today? (Listen to their tone of voice.)

4. Purpose:
   *I'm calling to let you know that we missed you at our last small group
   meeting. We care about you and your family, and I wanted to know if
   I could pray with you about any particular needs. (If a prayer concern
   is mentioned, write it down.)*

5. Prayer:
   *Would it be all right if we prayed together right now
   for_____(the prayer request)?*

Let's pray, "Heavenly Father, thank you for your love today. Thank you for your power to do all things…nothing is impossible with you. In full assurance of faith we put_____into your loving hands. We ask for_____(the prayer request) and we expect good things to happen. Lord, thank you for hearing us and we give you praise. In Jesus' name, amen."

6. Close the conversation:
    Thank you so much for taking time to talk to me. I look forward to talking to you again.
    Good bye.

MINISTRY ACTIVITY: CALL THOSE ON YOUR CARE LIST

After reviewing the key principles with your equipper, make at least five ministry phone calls to people on your Care List (see lesson, A Care List and Appendix D: Ministry Contact Records). Remember, maintain an attitude of prayer throughout your time of calling. Keep the phone calls short, and show them that you care!

1. Time:

2. Date:

3. Names of people called:

REFLECTION AND EVALUATION

1. What things went well?

2. What did you enjoy most about this ministry activity?

3. What will you do differently next time?

EFFECTIVE LISTENING

KEY VERSE: JAMES 1:19

"My dear brothers, take note of this: Everyone should be quick to listen, slow to speak and slow to become angry."

INTRODUCTION

One of the greatest gifts that one person can offer to another is effective listening. However, conversations can often be described as two people trying to talk with the least amount of listening possible.

1. Discuss a personal experience you have had when someone really demonstrated their concern for you by effectively listening to your thoughts and concerns.

2. Discuss why it is important to be an effective listener.

KEY PRINCIPLES

WHAT IS LISTENING?

1. It is more than just waiting for your turn to speak.

2. It is seeking to understand what the speaker is trying to communicate.

3. It is showing respect, love and concern for another person.

4. It is trying to see life through the eyes of the other person.

WHY IS EFFECTIVE LISTENING IMPORTANT?

1. It demonstrates respect for the speaker.

2. It shows that you are interested in the speaker.

3. It shows that you are not trying to change, evaluate or argue with the other person.

4. It allows you to demonstrate that you really care.

5. It keeps you from looking foolish by speaking before you've heard all the information. (Proverbs 18:13)

EVALUATE YOUR LISTENING SKILLS

1. Communication involves speaking and listening. However, most people put more energy and effort in delivering what they have to say than in receiving what someone else wants them to hear. Which of the following best represents your listening style?

    ❏ Listening in order to reply: "When I'm not speaking, I'm thinking about what I want to say."
    ❏ Listening in order to understand: "I'm usually seeking to understand the ideas and feelings of others."

2. Here is another way to evaluate your listening style. Which of the following best describes you?
    ❏ Ignoring – not really listening at all.
    ❏ Pretend Listening – "Yeah. Uh-huh. Right. Sure."
    ❏ Selective Listening – hearing only certain parts of the conversation.
    ❏ Active Listening – hearing the words that are being said.
    ❏ Effective Listening – trying to understanding both the words and the feelings behind them.

HOW TO LISTEN MORE EFFECTIVELY

1. Get Ready — Prepare yourself and your setting:
   a. Face the person.
   b. Make frequent eye contact. Maintaining good eye contact helps to build trust.
   c. Show interest by your body language and facial expressions. For example, leaning forward conveys a sense of concern or interest while leaning back with arms crossed conveys a sense of doubt and mistrust.
   d. Get rid of distractions. Turn off the radio or television. Avoid annoying habits such as tapping a pencil, looking at your watch or taking your ring on and off. Such distractions convey a lack of attention and interest.

2. Get Set — Review this mental checklist of things to avoid:
   a. Don't get impatient or discouraged. If you do not have time to listen adequately, then set a time when you can.
   b. Don't mind-read. Try to listen without jumping to conclusions or assuming that you know what they will say.
   c. Don't interrupt. Stop talking and allow the other person to complete a whole thought.
   d. Don't offer advice until asked. Unwanted advice is endured but not welcomed, received or applied.

3. Go — Take the challenge to listen effectively:
   a. **Listen attentively** to what the person is saying. When you sense that someone is expressing ideas that they have strong feelings about, pay very close attention and be ready to repeat in your own words what you have heard.
   b. **Summarize** or paraphrase what you've heard.
      1) Recognize the ideas. When the speaker has completed a thought try to summarize what you've heard by paraphrasing it, **"What I hear you saying is. . . ."**
      2) Recognize and identify emotions. You can also sense and see emotions through their body language and tone of voice. When possible, add these observations to your paraphrase, **". . . I sense you're feeling _____."**
   c. **Ask for clarification** and additional information. Ask ques-

tions if anything is unclear, but continue to discover the speaker's point of view. Use some of the following questions:

1) **"Did I understand what you were trying to say?"**
2) **"Is there more that you would like to share?"**
3) **"How do you feel about what you have shared?"**
4) **"I'm not sure that I understood what you were saying, could you tell me that again?"**

MINISTRY ACTIVITY: PRACTICE EFFECTIVE LISTENING. Review the
principles listed above. Then practice effective listening with someone from your Care List or role play effective listening with your equipper.

1. Time:

2. Date:

3. Person with whom you met:

REFLECTION AND EVALUATION

1. What things went well?

2. What did you enjoy most about this ministry activity?

3. What will you do differently next time that will help you listen more effectively?

PRAYER MINISTRY

KEY VERSES: JAMES 5:13-16

"Is any one of you in trouble? He should pray. Is anyone happy? Let him sing songs of praise. Is any one of you sick? He should call the elders of the church to pray over him and anoint him with oil in the name of the Lord. And the prayer offered in faith will make the sick person well; the Lord will raise him up. If he has sinned, he will be forgiven. Therefore, confess your sins to each other and pray for each other so that you may be healed. The prayer of a righteous man is powerful and effective."

INTRODUCTION

Prayer is the heart of ministry and we do not accomplish anything of lasting spiritual significance without prayer.

1. Discuss the personal experiences you have had praying for the needs of others. Also, talk about when you have had someone pray with you for a personal need.

2. Discuss why it is important to base your personal ministry on the foundation of prayer.

KEY PRINCIPLES

PREPARING YOURSELF TO PRAY

1. Keep your relationship with God clear and up-to-date:
   a. No unconfessed sin (1 John 1:9).
   b. Ask the Holy Spirit to reveal any sinful actions, thoughts or attitudes that are unpleasing to Him.

    c.   Have regular times of worship, praise and study of God's Word.

2.   Keep your relationships with others clear and up-to-date:
    a.   Let your actions demonstrate unconditional love and acceptance. As it has been said, "People do not care how much you know, until they know how much you care" (1 John 3:18).
    b.   Determine to forgive everyone who sins against you (Matthew 6:14-15; 18:21-35).
    c.   Seek to be reconciled to those who have something against you (Matthew 5:23-24).

PRAYING FOR PEOPLE (INTERCESSORY PRAYER MINISTRY)

1.   Understand the basics of Intercessory Prayer.
    a.   What is intercession? To intercede means to plead or make a request on behalf of individuals or groups. Intercessory prayer, therefore, is pleading or making requests to God on behalf of individuals or groups.
    b.   How does a person intercede in prayer?
        1)   Identify the need.
        2)   Seek to understand God's heart for the situation.
        3)   Identify scripture that addresses the need.
        4)   Pray for the need in light of God's will and His Word.[1]

2.   Pray for those on your Care List:
    a.   Those who attend your small group.
    b.   Those who are prospects for your small group.
    c.   Pray for those in your "circle of influence," those in whom you have taken a spiritual interest:
        1)   Neighbors
        2)   Family
        3)   Co-workers

3.   Pray for the ministry of your local church:
    a.   Pastors and support staff
    b.   Lay leaders
    c.   Ministry volunteers

    d.   Children and youth
    e.   Members
    f.   Those who God wants to bring into relationship with Him.

4.   Pray for those in authority:
    a.   Local and State government.
    b.   National government leaders.
    c.   Leaders of other nations.

PRAYING WITH PEOPLE (PERSONAL PRAYER MINISTRY)

1.   Tune into the needs of people (see the lesson, Effective Listening):
    a.   "Listen" with your eyes. What is their body language communicating?
    b.   Listen attentively and summarize what you've heard.
    c.   Avoid counseling or advising. Remember the goal is to pray for the need that is being expressed.

2.   Help them define the need.
    a.   Determine the type of need:
       1)   Is it physical?
       2)   Is it financial?
       3)   Is it spiritual?
       4)   Is it emotional
       5)   Is it relational?
    b.   Ask clarifying questions:
       1)   What is it that you want God to do for you?
       2)   How can I pray for you right now?

3.   Ask if you may pray together right now:
    a.   Offer a brief prayer for their personal need.
    b.   Give them the opportunity to pray for their need.
    c.   Apply scriptures to the need by praying or quoting them as God brings them to mind.
    d.   Thank God for hearing and answering your prayer.

MINISTRY ACTIVITY: PRAY FOR AND WITH SOMEONE FROM YOUR CARE LIST. Pray for the needs of those on your Care List and meet with one person from your Care List to pray with them for a specific need.

1. Time:

2. Date:

3. Person for whom and with whom you prayed:

REFLECTION AND EVALUATION

1. What things went well?

2. What did you enjoy most about this ministry activity?

3. What will you do differently next time?

RESOURCES

Copeland, Germaine. *A Call To Prayer: Intercession in Action.*
    Tulsa OK: Harrison House, 1991.
*Prayers that Avail Much: An Intercessor's Handbook of Scriptural
    Prayers, Vol. 1.* Tulsa OK: Harrison House, 1989.
*Prayers that Avail Much: An Intercessor's Handbook of Scriptural
    Prayers, Vol. 2.* Tulsa OK: Harrison House, 1989, 1991.

PROVIDING CARE

KEY VERSES: ROMANS 12:9-13

"Love must be sincere. . . . Be devoted to one another in brotherly love. Honor one another above yourselves. Never be lacking in zeal, but keep your spiritual fervor, serving the Lord. Share with God's people who are in need. Practice hospitality."

INTRODUCTION

All of us have opportunities to put Christ's love in action by showing loving, caring behavior to those in our sphere of influence; those in whom we have taken a spiritual interest in.

1. Discuss any personal experiences you have had in making personal, caring contact with someone in whom you have taken a spiritual interest.

2. Discuss why this ministry skill is so important for all of us to put into practice, regardless of our giftedness.

KEY PRINCIPLES

Apply the following C.A.R.E. principles to those on your Care List:

C - CONTACT YOUR CARE LIST ON A REGULAR BASIS

1. Look for opportunities to show love and concern.
    a. Making regular contacts to build relationships is essential.
    b. Be aware of special life events for opportunities to show love and care: birthdays, anniversaries, promotions, graduations, births, achievements, honors, retirements etc.

    c.   Respond to crisis situations such as the death of a loved one, the loss of a job or financal hardships, broken relationships, sickness or hospitalization.

    d.   Affirm new commitments and spiritual decisions in the person's life and encourage or support them in their growth.

2.   Make an appropriate response or contact.[1] Select the action that is most appropriate for the individual situation. If you are not sure, ask a pastor or experienced care giver to guide you.

    a.   Phone calls — Make them brief and be considerate in your timing.

    b.   Personal notes and cards are always appreciated for special life events, crisis or to encourage and edify.

    c.   Give an invitation for dinner, desert, a luncheon appointment or getting together for coffee.

    d.   Invite the person to join you in a small group or a one-to-one discipleship meeting.

    e.   Home visits — Short home visits can be appropriate if the person is sick, shut-in or if they have invited you to visit them. Always call first to schedule the appointment.

A - ACCEPT SPIRITUAL RESPONSIBILITY

1.   Be informed: Know what is happening in the lives of those with whom you have a spiritual interest.

2.   Be available: The most important thing you can do is to just show up. 50-75% of ministry is just being there.

3.   Be sensitive: Try to Minster in a way that meets their needs rather than yours. Be aware of special circumstances and use good common sense.

4.   Be brief: Try to keep your visits and phone calls brief. A hospital or home visit should be no more than 15 minutes. Keep a phone call five to seven minutes long unless the person requests to talk longer.

5.   Be positive.

6.   Be open: Ask how you can be of help.

7.   Be confident: You don't have to have all the answers, just affirm your love and support.

8.   Be a listener: Active listening is loving, do not give advice (see lesson, Effective Listening).

R - RESPOND TO NEEDS

1.   A practical way to provide care is by responding to the needs in peoples lives.
     a.   Take a meal to a family where a parent has been recently hospitalized or is too ill to cook.
     b.   Provide child care in a crisis situation.
     c.   Pray with the person when they express a need (see lesson, Prayer Ministry).
     d.   Give a helping hand with a project.
     e.   Mow the lawn for an elderly person.
     f.   Invite them over for dinner.
     g.   Sit with them in church.
     h.   Visit them in the hospital (see lesson, Hospital Visitation).

2.   Do to others what you would have them do to you (Matthew 7:12). Put yourself in that person's situation. There are many creative ways you can serve.

E - ENCOURAGE AND EDIFY
Everyone needs encouragement, edification (building up) and appreciation.

1.   Encourage them: Give a positive word, scripture, note, call or contact to lift the person and help them feel better.

2.   Edify them: To edify means to instruct or improve spiritually. Look for ways to build that person up in their spiritual life.
     a.   Pray with them.
     b.   Meet with them for discipleship.[2]

    c.   Invite them to join you at a small group meeting.

    d.   Give them a Christian book or tape that has helped you.

3.   Appreciate them: Nothing builds a person up more than a sincere word of thanks.

MINISTRY ACTIVITY: MAKE A CARE CONTACT.

Review the principles of C.A.R.E. listed above. Review the names of those on your Care List. Decide who you should contact and what type of care contact would be most appropriate.

1. Time:

2. Date:

3. Who did you contact and in what way did you provide care?

REFLECTION AND EVALUATION

1. What things went well?

2. What did you enjoy most about your care contact?

3. What will you do differently next time?

HOSPITAL VISITATION

KEY VERSES: Matthew 25:35-36

"For I was hungry and you gave me something to eat, I was thirsty and you gave me something to drink, I was a stranger and you invited me in, I needed clothes and you clothed me, I was sick and you looked after me, I was in prison and you came to visit me."

INTRODUCTION

Often a hospital is an uncomfortable place for patients and for those who visit them.

1. Discuss any personal experiences you have had either as a patient or in visiting the sick and hospitalized.

2. Discuss why you think it is important and helpful to visit those who are sick and hospitalized.

KEY PRINCIPLES

SOME THINGS "TO DO" IN HOSPITAL VISITATION

1. Keep the visit short (five to 10 minutes is usually enough).

2. If the person is asleep, allow them to continue sleeping. Write a note and leave it where they will see it when they awake.

3. If you are not acquainted with the patient, introduce yourself in the following way:
    a. Give them your name and the name of your church.
    b. Tell them how you were referred (a friend, a pastor at your church, etc.).

4. Consider your appearance and personal hygiene.
    a. Wear appropriate clothing.
    b . Use breath freshener and deodorant.
    c. Avoid perfumes and colognes as they can be nauseating to those who are ill.
    d. Wash you hands before and after visiting.

5. Keep a smile on your face and be pleasant and cheerful.

6. Be friendly and positive.

7. Ask if there is anything that you can do for the patient such as an errand, a phone call, or write a letter or note.

8. Ask if you can read from the Bible:
    a. Choose a passage that brings encouragement or comfort (see Selected Scriptures, Appendix D: Ministry Contact Records).
    b. Read slowly and clearly.
    c. Use a Bible that has modern language which is easy to listen to and understand.

9. Ask if you can pray with the patient:
    a. Make your prayer personal and short.
    b. Lightly touch the patient.

10. Continue to remember the patient by praying and contacting them in person, by phone or letter.

11. Inform the patient's church and Pastor regarding your visit and the condition of the patient.

12. Stand where the patient can see you without difficulty. Avoid causing them to move their head or body in order to see you.

SOME "DON'TS" FOR HOSPITAL VISITATION

1. Don't interrupt a patient's meal; allow it to be eaten while it is still hot.

2. As a rule, do not mention the patient's illness unless they wish to talk about it.

3. Sometimes after surgery, a person is unable to talk. Don't ask questions or try to gain a response, instead:
    a. Tell why you came to visit.
    b. Briefly read the Bible and pray.

4. Do not touch the patient's bed. Do not bump it, sit on it or hold onto the railings.

5. Never talk about another person you knew who had a similar medical problem, especially if that person died or was permanently disabled.

6. Don't talk about negative things such as news headlines, personal problems or difficulties within the church.

7. Don't disrupt the work of nurses or doctors. Leave the room when they are tending the patient. Also, brag on the kind of care the people receive in that particular hospital.

8. Don't leave tracts and evangelistic literature without the permission of the patient. If in doubt, check with the hospital chaplain's office.

MINISTRY ACTIVITY: VISIT SOMEONE WHO IS IN THE HOSPITAL.

Together, review the "Do's" and "Don'ts" listed above. Then, visit one or more patients who are hospitalized. If you are visiting two or more patients during one trip, allow the equipper to demonstrate how to do a hospital visit with the first patient, then allow the apprentice to take the lead during a second hospital visit.

1. Time:

2. Date:

3. What patients were visited?

REFLECTION AND EVALUATION

1. What things went well?

2. What did you enjoy most about this ministry activity?

3. What will you do differently next time?

RESOURCES

1. A Bible.
2. A card which can be left if the patient is out of the room or asleep at the time of your visit.
3. Booklets that will bring comfort.

LOVE IN ACTION

KEY VERSES: 1 JOHN 3:16-18

"This is how we know what love is: Jesus Christ laid down his life for us. And we ought to lay down our lives for our brothers. If anyone has material possessions and sees his brother in need but has no pity on him, how can the love of God be in him? Dear children, let us not love with words or tongue but with actions and in truth."

INTRODUCTION

Love in action involves looking for ways to serve others through acts of love and deeds of kindness. It means connecting with people and meeting them at their point of need. By doing so, you are being a living witness of love.

1. Discuss any personal experiences you have had in demonstrating Christian love by meeting someone's specific need.

2. Discuss why you think it is important to do deeds of love and acts of kindness to Christians as well as the unchurched.

KEY PRINCIPLES

WHO SHOULD YOU HELP?

Jesus said, "Love your neighbor as yourself." A religious leader trying to justify himself asked, "And who is my neighbor?" Jesus answered by telling a story (Luke 10:25-37). A Samaritan saw a man who had been beaten and robbed. The good Samaritan had compassion on the injured man and took specific steps to meet his needs. In this parable, Jesus illustrated that your neighbor can be anyone, anywhere who needs the help you can offer.

1. Who are the Christians that you can help?
   a. Your church family and small group members.
   b. Friends of church families and small group prospects.

2. Who are the unchurched people that you can help?
   a. Your immediate family.
   b. Friends and neighbors.
   c. People at work or school.
   d. People in the community.

HOW TO BE A LIVING WITNESS OF LOVE

One of the most exciting, effective and rewarding ways to show the love of Jesus to unchurched people is to seek to serve them at their point of need. Rather than asking something from them you are offering them help, hope and love without obligation. You are showing the love of Jesus, who said, "For even the Son of Man did not come to be served, but to serve, and to give his life as a ransom for many" (Mark 10:45).

1. Pray for the unchurched people that God has placed in your life.

2. Offer unconditional love and acceptance. Don't require that they change before you extend your love and friendship.

3. Develop a closer relationship with them.
   a. Look for common ground: interests, hobbies, sports or work.
   b. Spend time together socially:
      1) Work together on household projects or automobiles.
      2) Invite them for dinner or dessert.
      3) Go out together to a concert or sporting event.

4. Seek to identify felt needs in their life. Are there financial, emotional, physical, spiritual or relational needs?

5. Offer to pray for their specific needs.
   a. Let them know that you have been praying for them.
   b. Offer to pray with them as well.

6. Take the initiative to help meet their needs:
   a. Meet the need personally, whenever possible.
   b. Seek help from your small group, church or others as needed.

HOW TO HELP THOSE IN NEED

You will usually find out about a person's needs from another friend or by your careful observation. However, as you build a trusting relationship, you may even be asked for help. Whatever way you come to know about a person in need, here are some steps to consider in putting your love into action.

1. Accept the person right where they are. True love is not conditional.

2. Listen to their story:
    a. Gather information.
    b. Don't make assumptions or try to read their mind.
    c. Share their pain with true concern and love.
    d. Be shock proof.
    e. Relate your own hurts and challenges when appropriate.

3. Identify their need:
    a. Ask specifically what they need.
    b. Ask what it is they would like done regarding their need.

4. Determine if you should help:
    a. Discern the cause of the need. Learn to discern what the need is and why the need exists. Are the needs a result of rebellion, disobedience, ignorance, neglect, immorality, financial set-backs, the cruelty of others?
    b. Don't do for others what they should do for themselves. Giving help when someone needs to take responsibility is ultimately a hindrance (1 Thessalonians 4:9-11; 2 Thessalonians 3:10).

5. Determine how you can help. Take an inventory of what you have available personally, through your small group, through your church and in your community:
    a. Donate food, clothing, furniture and household items.
    b. Offer transportation.
    c. Provide services to repair household items or vehicles.
    d. Offer to pray with and for them.
    e. Buy fuel for an automobile. Caution: In some states you

may be held liable for helping someone drive who doesn't have a current valid driver's license and insurance.
f. Provide food or medicine.
g. Offer to pay utility bills directly to the company.
h. Provide a listing of referral agencies for help or counseling.

6. Allow them to maintain their personal dignity and honor.
    a. Help them help themselves.
    b. Keep their need anonymous or as private as possible.

7. Get them connected with a small group for ongoing love and support. Find the type of small group that will best help them at this time: drug and alcohol support groups, marriage skills and enrichment, divorce recovery, grief recovery, parenting skills and support, Bible discussion groups or basic discipleship studies.

MINISTRY ACTIVITY: HELP SOMEONE BY MEETING A SPECIFIC NEED.

Review the names of those on your Care List (see lesson, A Care List, and Appendix D: Ministry Contact Records). Identify several people from your Care List who have specific needs. Then, select one person from your list who you will seek to show "love in action" by meeting their specific need.

1. Time:

2. Date:

3. Describe the need and how it was met:

REFLECTION AND EVALUATION

1. What things went well?

2. What did you enjoy most about this ministry activity?

3. What will you do differently next time?

INTRODUCING PEOPLE TO JESUS CHRIST

KEY VERSES: 2 CORINTHIANS 5:20-21

"We are therefore Christ's ambassadors, as though God were making his appeal through us. We implore you on Christ's behalf: Be reconciled to God. God made him who has no sin to be sin for us, so that in him we might become the righteousness of God."

INTRODUCTION

By taking the initiative to meet with someone who is spiritually hungry, you can be used by God to introduce that person to Jesus. When a person is "introduced" to Jesus they will never be the same. Their world view changes. Their character changes! Life itself changes! God has chosen you to be an "ambassador" for Christ, He is ready to use you to "introduce" people to Jesus.

1. Discuss any personal experiences you have had in talking to someone about how to receive Jesus Christ as their personal Savior.

2. Discuss why you think it's important to introduce people to Jesus.

KEY PRINCIPLES

PERSONAL PREPARATION

1. Pray, Pray, Pray, Pray, and Pray some more.
   a. Pray before you decide to talk to someone about Jesus.
   b. Pray while you are talking to someone about Jesus.

c.   Pray when you have finished your conversation.

2.   Place your confidence in the Holy Spirit, not yourself:
     a.   Realize that the Holy Spirit is the one who convicts of sin
          (John 16:8-9).
     b.   Rely on the Holy Spirit, who empowers, teaches and brings
          things to your remembrance while you are introducing
          someone to Jesus (John 14:26).
     c.   Remember that the Holy Spirit is in control
          (Ephesians 5:18).

3.   Prepare your testimony. Write out your testimony. It should take
     no longer than three minutes to tell. Rehearse your testimony
     with a trusted friend who will critique you honestly (see
     Preparing a Personal Testimony, Appendix D: Ministry Contact
     Records). A testimony has three parts:
     a.   Before you met Jesus: "Before I met Jesus I was fearful. I was
          not very secure."
     b.   How you met Jesus: "Then one day I met Jesus when a friend
          of mine shared four spiritual principles with me and invited
          me to accept Jesus personally."
     c.   After you met Jesus: "Now my life is peaceful because I know
          He loves me and will take care of me."

4.   Memorize the two diagnostic questions developed by Dr. D. James
     Kennedy, creator of Evangelism Explosion:[1]
     a.   "Have you come to the place in your spiritual life where you
          know for certain that if you were to die today you would go
          to heaven, or is that something you would say you are still
          working on?"
     b.   "Suppose that you were to die tonight and stand before God
          and He were to say to you, 'Why should I let you into my
          heaven?' What would you say?"

5.   Become comfortable with a simple presentation of how to know
     Jesus personally (see Appendix D: Ministry Contact Records).

INTRODUCING JESUS TO SOMEONE

The following steps are guidelines for making a personal visit to talk
to someone about how to know Jesus Christ as their personal Savior.

1. Call and make an appointment or plan a time to visit when you think you would be well received. Be sensitive.

2. Your Arrival:
   a. If you have scheduled an appointment, be on time.
   b. As soon as you park the car, move in a quiet and pleasant manner toward the door.

3. Build rapport:
   a. Establish a relationship quickly.
   b. Look for things of common interest.
   c. Talk about family pictures, collections, pets, decor and other general items of interest that catch your eye as you enter the home.

4. Ask open ended questions:
   a. Ask about family; ask "surface" questions in the beginning. This is not an investigation but a friendly introduction of yourself and Jesus.
   b. If they have visited your church, ask, "How did you discover our church?" "What did you enjoy most about your visit?"

5. When appropriate, turn the conversation to spiritual things. This can be done by talking about their church background, their interest in your church or any other indication of their interest in spiritual things. Encourage them to tell about their own spiritual life.

6. After they have talked about their spiritual journey, tell about yours:
   a. Share your personal testimony.
   b. Tell about what God is doing for you through your involvement in your local church.

7. Next, ask the two diagnostic questions.[2] The answers to these questions will alert you to the persons spiritual condition. Listen carefully to their answers.
   a. "Have you come to the place in your spiritual life where you know for certain that if you were to die today you would go to heaven, or is that something you would say you are still working on?"

    b.   "Suppose that you were to die tonight and stand before God and He were to say to you, 'Why should I let you into my heaven?' What would you say?"

8.   Present a simple explanation of how to know Jesus personally.
    a.   Ask permission to present this information.
    b.   If permission is not granted then politely move to another less personal subject before ending your visit. If appropriate, extend an invitation to meet again to talk about Jesus.

9.   Give an opportunity for the person to receive Jesus Christ as their Savior and friend. There is no way that you can adequately judge whether or not the person is ready to pray to receive Christ unless you give them a specific opportunity to do so. Many times someone, who previously appeared to be rather indifferent, will want to pray when they are given the definite opportunity to ask Jesus Christ to be the Savior and Lord of their life.

MINISTRY ACTIVITY: INTRODUCE SOMEONE TO JESUS

Practice presenting your personal testimony with your equipper. Then visit someone who needs to know how to become a Christian. You may call your Pastor for the name of someone to contact or visit someone on your Care List who needs to hear a clear presentation of the gospel of Jesus Christ.

1.   Time:
2.   Date:
3.   Person visited:

REFLECTION AND EVALUATION

1.   What things went well?

2.   What did you enjoy most about this ministry activity?

3.   What will you do differently next time?

HELPING NEW CHRISTIANS GROW

KEY VERSES: 1 PETER 2:2-3

"Like newborn babies, crave pure spiritual milk, so that by it you may grow up in your salvation, now that you have tasted that the Lord is good."

INTRODUCTION

When someone makes a spiritual commitment to follow Jesus Christ as their personal Lord and Savior, it is vital that they receive immediate care and follow-up. It can be compared to the care and attention needed after the birth of a new baby.

1. Discuss any personal experiences you have had in helping someone become established in their faith and walk with Jesus Christ.

2. Discuss why you think it is important to be prepared to help someone grow and mature after receiving Jesus Christ.

KEY PRINCIPLES

A new Christian needs someone who can help them become established and grow. The spiritual helper's role is to provide encouragement and support to the new believer, answer questions, explain the basics of Christian living and help the new Christian connect with the fundamentals of the faith and with other believers through a local church.

STEP 1: KEEP IN CLOSE CONTACT

Whenever you have helped someone make a decision to receive Christ into their life, it is important to do the following things:

1.   Exchange addresses and phone numbers.

2.   Set a time to get together again within the next few days.

3.   Make sure they have a copy of the Bible (or New Testament).

4.   Help them identify a church were they will feel comfortable attending the following Sunday.

STEP 2: HELP THEM BECOME ESTABLISHED

Your primary goal is to help the new Christian become established in their new faith and find assurance of their salvation through God's promises in His Word. Here is what you might do:

1.   Review the basic plan of salvation.

2.   Answer any questions that the new believer may have.

3.   Read 1 John 5:11-13. Ask: "According to this scripture, in whom is eternal life found?" "Who has eternal life?" "If you were to die tonight, do you know that you would spend eternity with God?"

4.   Discuss the following truths about believers:
     a.   Forgiven (Ephesians 1:7; Acts 10:43).
     b.   Justified (Romans 3:28; Acts 13:39).
     c.   A new creation (2 Corinthians 5:17).
     d.   A temple of God's Spirit (1 Corinthians 6:19; Ephesians 1:13; 4:30).
     e.   Delivered from condemnation (Romans 8:1; 1 John 5:24).

5.   Encourage the new believer to continue reading daily in the New Testament (perhaps beginning wtih the Gospel of John). Discuss any insights or questions this reading has brought up.

6.   Help the new believer learn how to deal with feelings of doubt:
     a.   Point out that feelings change based on circumstances.
     b.   Remind them that followers of Christ live by faith. Christians place their trust in what God has declared.
     c.   God's truth and promises do not change even when we have doubts and fears.

STEP 3: HELP THE NEW CHRISTIAN GROW IN FELLOWSHIP AND FAITH.

Through one-on-one meetings, small groups, classes for new
Christians and other growth opportunities, see that the new believer
is connected in a church and learning basic spiritual skills.

1. Growing In Fellowship: A fireplace illustrates the need for "close
   fellowship"; Several logs burn brightly together, but put one aside
   on the cold hearth and the fire goes out. So it is with your relationship with Christ. You need to remain in close contact with
   other Christians who are also "on fire" for Jesus Christ. Every
   Christian needs strong, supportive relationships with other
   Christians. This is accomplished in several ways. In which of
   the following ways is the new believer connected in the body of
   Christ?
   a. A weekly worship celebration service.
   b. A new christian's class.
   c. A small group.
   d. One-to-one discipleship.

2. Growing In Faith: Spiritual growth also requires gaining knowledge of God's truth and applying it to daily life. The basic areas
   for helping a Christian mature in their faith are represented by
   the twelve lessons contained in the book *Steps Toward Spiritual
   Growth*:
   a. Assurance of Salvation
   b. Victory Over Sin and Temptation
   c. Prayer
   d. The Bible — God's Word
   e. Sharing Your Faith
   f. Fellowship
   g. The Attributes of God
   h. The Person of Jesus
   i. The Holy Spirit
   j. Stewardship
   k. Obedience
   l. Spiritual Gifts

MINISTRY ACTIVITY: SEEK TO HELP A NEW CHRISTIAN BECOME ESTABLISHED IN THEIR FAITH AND IN FELLOWSHIP WITH OTHER CHRISTIANS

Meet with someone who has recently made a commitment for Christ and help them become established in their faith and in fellowship with other Christians. Use the basic steps listed above as a guide to assess how this person is doing and what additional follow-up needs to be done. Meet with this person and be prepared to help them connect with the people and resources that they need to grow as a new Christian.

1. Time:

2. Date:

3. Name of the new Christian that was contacted:

REFLECTION AND EVALUATION

1. What things went well?

2. What did you enjoy most about this ministry activity?

3. What will you do differently next time?

APPENDIX A
SMALL GROUP
PLANNING SHEET

1. **Location** where the group will meet:

   Address:_____

   _____

2. **Day of meeting:**_____ **Time:**_____

   Starting Date:_____

   Length of Small Group: ❏ Weeks ❏ Months ❏ On-going

3. **Type of small group:**
   __ Men's   __ Couples   __ Mature Adults
   __ Women's   __ Young Adults   __ Singles
   __ Mixed Adult   __ Support/Recovery __ Workplace
   __ Other:_____

4. **Description of lesson materials:**
   __ Standard Small Group Lesson
   __ Men's Small Group Lesson
   __ Other (please explain):_____

5. **Leadership Team:**

   Leader:_____ phone #:_____

   Assistant:_____ phone #:_____

   Host:_____ phone #:_____

6. **Invitation list:** Create a prospect list of those you wish to attend the group. Consider those within your circle of influence: family, neighbors, friends at work, church, school, clubs or other organizations in which you participate.

Name   **Phone**

_____

_____

_____

_____

_____

_____

_____

_____

_____

_____

_____

_____

_____

_____

_____

_____

_____

_____

_____

_____

APPENDIX B

SMALL GROUP MEETING CHECKLIST

PREPARE FOR THE MEETING

SET-UP AND PREPARATION
- ❑ Arrive 20 minutes before meeting.
- ❑ Pray with the leadership team.
- ❑ Try to make the setting free of interruptions.
- ❑ Create an uplifting setting with good lighting.
- ❑ Arrange seating in a circle and have extra chairs available.
- ❑ Provide for drinks and refreshments.
- ❑ Have copies of the discussion guide ready to distribute.
- ❑ Have extra Bibles and pens available.

AS PEOPLE ARRIVE
- ❑ Greet arriving guests with warmth and hospitality.
- ❑ Offer refreshments prior to, during or after the meeting.
- ❑ Help the host create an atmosphere of love, warmth and acceptance.

PRESENT A BALANCED MEETING

SHARED LIFE (15 MINUTES) Determine which of the following components will be included and who will do them:
- ❑ Welcome and opening prayer.
- ❑ Introduction of guests.
- ❑ Fun ice breaker activities or questions.
- ❑ Testimonies or reports of answered prayer.
- ❑ Expressions of appreciation for one another.
- ❑ Worship through singing.
- ❑ Announcements.

CONVERSATIONAL PRAYER (10 MINUTES)

Conversational prayer is topical prayer. Prayer starters can include thanking God for what He has done; asking God to do something for a person within the group; praising God for who He is, etc. Review the guidelines below and determine who will direct the prayer time:

1. Praying conversationally simply means talking to God in an easy, natural conversation.
2. Each person should feel free to pray several times using short sentence prayers.
3. No one person should dominate the prayer time.
4. Several people should pray short sentences on each topic before changing to a new prayer focus.
5. No one should ever feel forced to pray out loud.
6. It is best not to go around the circle and take prayer requests but to have people speak out their requests as the group is praying conversationally.

BIBLE APPLICATION (30 MINUTES)

The goal of a small group is to apply the Bible to everyday life, learning to live in obedience to God. Evaluate your Bible Lesson using the following guidelines and decide who will lead the discussion:

❏ Start with an opener question which will point the conversation in the direction of the topic.
❏ Read the Bible passage and discuss the lesson.
❏ Can some questions only be answered by looking at the Bible?
❏ Are there thought questions which allow anyone to offer an opinion or perspective?
❏ Is there a closing question which helps group members apply the Bible lesson in their lives this week?

CLOSING CONVERSATIONAL PRAYER (FIVE MINUTES)

Close with conversational prayer (five minutes). The primary focus of this closing prayer is the application of Bible truths in the lives of group members: "Lord, help me this week to apply in my life what you have shown me in your Word today."

❏ Who will lead this closing prayer time?
❏ How will you close the prayer time?
❏ Will you use "The Lord's Prayer?"

APPENDIX C

GOOD GROUP DYNAMICS

SEATING ARRANGEMENTS CHECKLIST

❏ Sit in a Circle. Seating was arranged in a circle, allowing every one to feel included.

❏ Same Eye Level. Members of the group were seated at approximately the same eye level.

❏ Only One Extra Chair. Chairs were added as they were needed.

❏ Eye Contact. Everyone could see the other members of the group.

PRINCIPLES FOR GOOD GROUP DYNAMICS

Review the following principles and evaluate how well the group did in emulating these good group dynamics:

	Low				High
1. **Practice mutual edification.** Seek to build each other up. Affirm one another. Encourage everyone in the group. Make each person feel important. Let them know that their ideas and comments are valued.	1	2	3	4	5
2. **Respond lovingly to a need expressed.** . . . immediately. Pray immediately when a need is expressed. Don't make a list of prayer requests before you start praying, pray when the first need is expressed.	1	2	3	4	5
3. **The leader is a facilitator** not the authority or teacher. The leader should not respond to every question but must allow the group members to give their input.	1	2	3	4	5
4. **Don't Hog — Don't Hide.** Everyone is encouraged to participate but no one is required to pray, read or speak. Everyone is encouraged to share but no one is allowed to dominate.	1	2	3	4	5

		Low			High

5. **Don't Go Around the Circle.** Avoid a pattern   1   2   3   4   5
    of reading, praying or sharing around the circle.
    This causes people to feel obligated to participate.

6. **Handle problem people away from the group**   1   2   3   4   5
    on a one-to-one basis. No dumping permitted.
    Avoid focusing advise on just one member of
    the group.

7. **No Gossip.** Don't allow people to confess   1   2   3   4   5
    anyone else's faults but their own. Don't talk
    about people outside the group. Focus on
    helping those in the group by asking "How
    can we pray for you?"

8. **Don't allow doctrinal discussion that is**   1   2   3   4   5
    divisive or argumentative.

9. **Present a balanced small group meeting.**   1   2   3   4   5
    Make it a priority to balance the three
    necessary elements for an effective meeting:
    Shared Life (15 minutes) Bible Application
    (30 minutes) and Conversational Prayer
    (15 minutes).

DIAGRAM THE GROUP INTERACTION

Diagram the groups discussion by placing an "L" for the location of
the leader and an "X" to represent where each group member is seated. Draw arrows to indicate who has talked and to whom they were
speaking. Continue this through the Shared Life and Bible Application portions of the group meeting. Ideally you will have lines and
arrows criss-crossing in every directions in your diagram indicating a
broad participation with no one person dominating the discussion.

Diagram   **Sample**

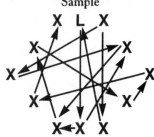

APPENDIX D

MINISTRY CONTACT RECORDS

A JOURNAL FOR LAY PASTORS AND SMALL GROUP LEADERS

This ministry tool serves as a care journal for lay pastors and small group leaders. It assists them in providing meaningful personal ministry contacts to those attending their small group, prospects for their group and those who are in their personal circle of influence.

SECTION #1 - CARE LIST
Small Group Members
Small Group Prospects
Circle of Influence

SECTION #2 - A-Z MINISTRY CONTACT RECORDS
Ministry Contact Records Journal pages

SECTION #3 - RESOURCES
Sample Ministry Phone Calls
Referral List for Emergency Help and Counseling
How to Know Jesus Personally
Preparing a Personal Testimony
Selected Scriptures

TO ORDER MINISTRY CONTACT RECORDS
A complete copy of the *Ministry Contact Records* includes blank Ministry Contact Records journal pages and A to Z tabbed dividers for ring binders. It can be purchased separately from the publisher, Foundation of Hope, 11731 SE Stevens Road, Portland, OR 97266, 1-888-248-3545, 503-659-5683.

CARE LIST

WHAT IS A CARE LIST?

1. A Care List simply identifies the people for whom you have taken a spiritual interest. It is a key tool for building an effective personal ministry to others. It becomes a "personal action list" that gives specific focus regarding our desire for God to use us. It could be called an "opportunity list."

2. Build your Care List by praying for God's guidance. Your Care List can include the people who attend your small group, prospects for your small group, those in your circle of influence such as friends, family, neighbors and co-workers in whom you have a spiritual interest as well as people referred to you by your church.

3. Make regular contact with each person on your Care List. Take a spiritual interest for these people and pray for them regularly. Pray that God will work in the lives of each person on your list even if they can't or don't come to your small group or church. Find out specific needs in the person's life and seek to show the love of Jesus by meeting those needs.

THREE PARTS OF A CARE LIST

1. Small Group Members.

2. Small Group Prospects.

3   Your Circle Of Influence.

SMALL GROUP MEMBERS

Leader:_____ phone #:_____

Assistant:_____ phone #:_____

Host:_____ phone #:_____

Regular attenders:

Name	Phone

SMALL GROUP PROSPECTS

Develop a unique prospect list that fits your type of small group (men's, women's, couples, singles, mixed adult, etc.). Include the appropriate people from your personal circle of influence on this list. Have your small group leadership team add to this list. Ask your pastor or church leaders for names and referrals for your small group prospect list.

Generally speaking, there is a 3:1 ratio between the total number you are inviting and the average attendance of your group. If you want a group attendance of 10 people, you need to have 30 people on your small group prospect list.

Name   **Phone**

_____

_____

_____

_____

_____

_____

_____

_____

_____

_____

_____

_____

_____

_____

YOUR CIRCLE OF INFLUENCE

Those in your circle of influence include friends, family, neighbors
and co-workers in whom you have taken a spiritual interest. Pray
about who you should include. God will often lead you by giving you
a burden for or a special interest in certain people. Pray for these people and look for ways to serve them through acts of love and deeds of
kindness.

Name   **Phone**

_____

_____

_____

_____

_____

_____

_____

_____

_____

_____

_____

_____

_____

_____

_____

_____

_____

_____

_____

MINISTRY CONTACT RECORDS

LAST NAME:_____Anderson_____

First Name: __Jeff_____ Birthday:_____4/6_____

Spouse:_____Patty_____ Birthday:_____11/17_____

Child:_____Birthday:_____

Child:_____Birthday:_____

Address:_____13402 SE 87th Road_____

City:____Portland·_____ State:__OR__ Zip: 97265_____

Phone: (Hm)____792-0463_____ (Wk) 233-9065_____

FAX_____ Pager_____ E-mail_____

Small Group Prospect__x__   Church Attender__x__

Small Group Member____   Church Member ____

---------------------MINISTRY CONTACT RECORD--------------

DATE	COMMENTS
7-13	T s/w Patty. Prayed with her that her health would improve. Had bad cold.
8-3	T invitation to small group BBQ.
8-14	Jeff - back surgery at OHSU. Prayed with him at the hospital.
8-15	T Bz sent "get well" L. for Jeff.
8-16	s/w Patty at the small group. Her 1st visit.
8-17	Hospital visit. Jeff is recovering well from back surgery. Will come home this week
8-20	T LMRec

MINISTRY CONTACT RECORDS JOURNAL PAGES

Ministry Contact Records is a journal for lay pastors and small group leaders. One Ministry Contact Records journal page is created for every family unit. Each time there is a personal or ministry contact, a journal entry should be made to record important details from that contact. Each journal page is filed alphabetically in a ring binder using A to Z tabbed dividers. With this simple system you are able to keep track of important details and prayer requests for a larger number of people than you could by simply depending on your memory.

MINISTRY CONTACT RECORDS SHORTHAND

The following abbreviations will help conserve space on each journal page.

1XV	=	FIRST TIME VISITOR
2XV	=	SECOND TIME VISITOR
3XV	=	THIRD TIME VISITOR
RA	=	REGULAR ATTENDER (CHURCH)
M	=	MEMBER (CHURCH)
T	=	TELEPHONED
N/A	=	NO ANSWER
LMRec	=	LEFT MESSAGE ON RECORDER
S/W	=	SPOKE WITH…
N/P	=	NON-PUBLISHED PHONE NUMBER
Bz	=	BUSY
L	=	LETTER OR NOTE
SmGp	=	SMALL GROUP
CC	=	WORSHIP COMMUNICATION CARD

MINISTRY CONTACT RECORDS SAMPLE

The previous page is a sample journal entry which demonstrates the use of the shorthand. Blank journal pages with A to Z tabbed dividers are included in each copy of the *Ministry Contact Records* which can be purchased separately from the publisher, Foundation of Hope, 11731 SE Stevens Road, Portland, OR 97266, 1-888-248-3545 or 503-659-5683.

SAMPLE MINISTRY PHONE CALLS

KEYS TO SUCCESSFUL MINISTRY BY PHONE

1. Ask God to give you the words to say.

2. Smile before and during your conversation. A smile can be "heard" over the phone.

3. When they answer the phone, introduce yourself, your ministry role (small group leader, etc.), and tell them the name of the church you represent.

4. Immediately, ask them if this is a convenient time to talk.

5. State the purpose of your call.

6. If they share a prayer request, ask if you may pray with them about it right now. If they allow you to, pray a short prayer with them about their concern.

7. At the close of your prayer, thank them for sharing, then end the conversation. Keep the phone call short. You want them to look forward to your next call.

8. Keep a record of the prayer request on a Ministry Contact Records journal sheet so that you can ask about it the next time that you call.

SAMPLE CALL FOR WELCOMING VISITORS

Hello,

This is_____, and
I'm a_____ (Lay Pastor, Small Group Leader, etc.) at
_____Church. May I speak with
_____?

Is this a convenient time to talk? (If yes, continue; if no, offer to call again)

I want you to know how pleased we are that you have attended our Sunday worship services.

What brought you to our church?

Do you have a church home?

Do you have any questions I could help you with?

I'd like to meet you this coming Sunday at church.

How about meeting me by the_____at about
_____?

I'll probably be wearing_____(give a helpful physical description of yourself).

I'm looking forward to meeting you.

Good bye.

NOTE: Keep conversation short and friendly.

SAMPLE CALL FOR SMALL GROUP PROSPECTS

Hello,

This is_____, and
I'm a_____(Lay Pastor, Small Group Leader, etc.) at
_____Church. May I speak with
_____?

Is this a convenient time to talk? (If yes, continue; if no, offer to call again)

Have you heard about our small groups?

One of the most rewarding things that I have experienced is the small group I attend every week on (day)_____at (time)_____.

I would love to have you visit our group. Do you think you might be able to come next_____at_____?
(Send a map/address/phone or offer a ride.)

Oh, that would be great.

I've enjoyed visiting with you,_____.

Optional close: I'd like to meet you this coming Sunday at church.

How about meeting me by the_____at about_____?

I'll probably be wearing_____(give a helpful physical description of yourself).

I'm looking forward to meeting you. Good bye.

NOTE: Keep conversation short and friendly.

SAMPLE CALL FOR FOLLOW-UP OF SPIRITUAL COMMITMENTS

Hello,

This is_____, and

I'm a_____ (Lay Pastor, Small Group Leader, etc.) at

_____Church. May I speak with

_____?

Is this a convenient time to talk? (If yes, continue; if no, offer to call again)

I understand that you have recently made some spiritual commitments to Jesus Christ and I wanted you to know I've been praying for you!

Could you tell me about what God has been doing in your life?

Do you have any questions I could help you with?

Have you heard about the_____class (New Christians Class, etc.) It's a special class offered for new and growing Christians that meets every Sunday at_____? It's very helpful. You'll be reviewing the basics of the Christian life. I know you'd benefit from it. It's an on-going class and you can start this Sunday.

Another way to really help you grow is to be part of a small group. It's one of the most rewarding things that's ever happened in my life. My small group meets every_____ at_____.
Would you like to be my guest at the group this week? (Send a map/address/phone or offer a ride.)

Great!

Optional prayer:

"Heavenly Father, thank you for all that You have done in_____'s life.

I pray that_____will sense Your presence as he/she faces the circumstances of life with You as Savior and Lord.

Help_____to be faithful in reading Your Word and talking with You daily in prayer. Give_____ the wisdom to know Your will and the courage to do it, I pray.

We love You, Lord, and we thank You for all that You have done. In Jesus' name we pray, Amen."

SAMPLE CALL FOR FOLLOW-UP OF A PRAYER REQUEST

Hello,

This is_____, and

I'm a_____ (Lay Pastor, Small Group Leader, etc.) at

_____Church. May I speak with

_____?

Is this a convenient time to talk? (If yes, continue; if no, offer to call again)

How are you doing today?

I received the prayer request that you submitted and I wanted you to know I've been praying for that request.

How can I pray for you today regarding_____(the prayer request)? I know that God is interested in your concerns.

Would it be all right if we had a prayer together right now?

Let's pray.

(SAMPLE:) "Heavenly Father, thank You for Your love today. Thank You for Your power to do all things...nothing is impossible with You.

In full assurance of faith we put_____into Your loving hands. We ask for Your divine help regarding _____ (the prayer request) and we wait expectantly upon You.

Lord, thank You for hearing us and we give You praise.

In Jesus' name, Amen."

REFERRAL LIST FOR EMERGENCY HELP AND COUNSELING
(SAMPLE FORMAT)

24-HOUR CRISIS HOTLINES

Clackamas County Crisis Line	555-0000
Metro-Crisis Intervention	223-0000
Washington County Crisis Intervention	648-0000
City of Tigard	248-0000
Vancouver Crisis Line	696-0000
Tom Jackson, Mental Health Counselor	226-0000
(Private) Welfare Clients	224-0000

EMERGENCY ASSISTANCE

Clackamas County	655-0000
Multnomah County (United Way)	222-0000

RECOVERY PROGRAMS (ALCOHOL & DRUGS)

New Day Center	231-0000
Teen Challenge	259-0000
Milwaukie Hospital (Dr. Jim Gallon)	653-0000

DETOX-ALCOHOL

Hoover Memorial Center	248-0000
Depot Center	223-0000
S.M.A.R.T. (Vancouver)	696-0000

DETOX-DRUGS

Drug Treatment Services (for referral)	239-0000

PARENTS SUPPORT GROUP (ALCOHOL AND DRUG ABUSE)

Vancouver Tough Love   574-0000

CHILD ABUSE

C.S.D. 24-Hour Hotline   238-0000
Vancouver 24-Hour Hotline   696-0000

PREGNANCY/ABORTION

Birthright Center   249-0000
Right to Life   245-0000
White Shield Home   226-4053

WOMEN'S SHELTERS

N.E. Portland (Brentwood House)   281-0000
N.W. Portland (Ravel House)   222-0000
Clackamas County (Evergreen House)   654-0000
Washington County (Hillsboro)   640-0000

HOUSING

Salvation Army   226-0000
Harbor Lights   223-0000

MARRIAGE COUNSELING

Fred Warner — Counselor   897-0000
Heart-to-Heart Counseling Center   299-0000

HOW TO KNOW JESUS PERSONALLY
(A SIMPLE PLAN OF SALVATION)

PRESENT A SIMPLE PLAN OF SALVATION: Review the ABCs of Salvation:

1. **ADMIT** your need. You are separated from God because of sin. Repent from your sin and turn to God. (Romans 3:23, 6:23)

2. **BELIEVE** in Jesus Christ. He is God's only provision for restoring the relationship with God that your sin has broken. Acknowledge that He is God, that He died for your sins and that He has risen victorious over sin and death. (John 14:6; Acts 4:12; Romans 5:8)

3. **CONFESS** your sins and receive Jesus Christ as your personal Savior. By faith receive salvation, spiritual life and forgiveness of sins through trust in Jesus Christ. (Romans 10:9-10; John 1:12)

4. **DEDICATE** yourself to a life of obedience as a follower of Jesus Christ. Determine that you will seek to honor Christ as a faithful disciple. (Matthew 28:18-20)

OTHER SIMPLE PLANS

1. *"Have You Heard of the Four Spiritual Laws"* by Bill Bright. Available at Christians bookstores or from the publisher, New Life Publications, P.O. Box 593684, Orlando, FL 32859-3684

2. *"Steps To Peace With God"* by Billy Graham. Available at Christian bookstores or from the Billy Graham Evangelistic Association, P.O. Box 779, Minneapolis, MN 55440-0779.

PREPARING A PERSONAL TESTIMONY

Every Christian has a testimony worth telling. It is your personal experience of God's love and grace. It is a powerful and personal way to lift up Jesus Christ and bring glory to God. Your personal testimony should follow a simple three-point outline:

1. Before I met Jesus Christ I lived and thought this way (use about 20 - 30% of your time):

2. How I met Jesus Christ (be specific and spend 35-40% of your time on this):

3. After I met Jesus Christ, these positive changes took place (using 35-40% of your time, emphasize this point and also tell what Christ is doing in your life now):

SELECTED SCRIPTURES

ABORTION *For you created my inmost being; you knit me together in my mother's womb. I praise you because I am fearfully and wonderfully made; your works are wonderful, I know that full well. My frame was not hidden from you when I was made in the secret place. When I was woven together in the depths of the earth, your eyes saw my unformed body. All the days ordained for me were written in your book before one of them came to be.*
Psalm 139:13-16

See also: Psalm 127:3

ADULTERY *Marriage should be honored by all, and the marriage bed kept pure, for God will judge the adulterer and all the sexually immoral.*
Hebrews 13:4

See also: 1 Corinthians 7:3-4

ANGER *In your anger do not sin: Do not let the sun go down while you are still angry, and do not give the devil a foothold. . . . Get rid of all bitterness, rage and anger, brawling and slander, along with every form of malice. Be kind and compassionate to one another, forgiving each other, just as in Christ God forgave you.*   Ephesians 4:26-27, 31-32

See also: Proverbs 15:1
                 Proverbs 19:11
                 Proverbs 29:11
                 Colossians 3:8
                 James 1:19-20

ANXIETY (SEE FEAR) *Do not be anxious about anything, but in everything, by prayer and petition, with thanksgiving, present your requests to God. And the peace of God, which transcends all understanding, will guard your hearts and your minds in Christ Jesus.*   Philippians 4:6-7

See also: Psalm 34:4, 18
                 Psalm 42:5
                 Psalm 127:1-2
                 Matthew 6:25-27, 31, 33-34
                 1 Peter 5:7

ASSURANCE OF SALVATION *For it is by grace you have been saved,*
through faith — and this not from yourselves, it is the gift of God — not by
works, so that no one can boast.   Ephesians 2:8-9
    See also: John 1:12
                John 5:24
                2 Corinthians 5:17
                1 John 5:11-13

BAPTISM *Peter replied, "Repent and be baptized, every one of you, in the*
name of Jesus Christ for the forgiveness of your sins. And you will receive
the gift of the Holy Spirit."   Acts 2:38
    See also: Matthew 28:18-19
                Romans 6:1-11

BIBLE *All Scripture is God-breathed and is useful for teaching, rebuking,*
correcting and training in righteousness, so that the man of God may be
thoroughly equipped for every good work.   2 Timothy 3:16-17
    See also: Joshua 1:8
                Psalm 119:105
                Hebrews 4:12
                2 Peter 1:20-21

CHRISTIAN FELLOWSHIP *And let us consider how we may spur one*
another on toward love and good deeds. Let us not give up meeting togeth-
er, as some are in the habit of doing, but let us encourage one another —
and all the more as you see the Day approaching.   Hebrews 10:24-25
    See also: John 17:20-23
                Acts 2:44-47
                1 Corinthians 1:10
                Galatians 6:2, 9-10
                Ephesians 4:15-16
                Philippians 2:1-4
                Colossians 3:16
                1 John 1:7

CHRISTIAN LIVING *Then he said to them all: "If anyone would come*
after me, he must deny himself and take up his cross daily and follow me.
For whoever wants to save his life will lose it, but whoever loses his life for
me will save it. What good is it for a man to gain the whole world, and yet
lose or forfeit his very self?"   Luke 9:23-25

See also: Matthew 22:37-40
             Romans 6:11-14
             Ephesians 4:14-15, 22-24
             2 Timothy 2:15
             1 Peter 3:15
             2 Peter 3:18

COMFORT (SEE ANXIETY, DISCOURAGEMENT, FEAR, HOPE)

Do you not know? Have you not heard? The LORD is the everlasting God, the Creator of the ends of the earth. He will not grow tired or weary, and his understanding no one can fathom. He gives strength to the weary and increases the power of the weak. Even youths grow tired and weary, and young men stumble and fall; but those who hope in the LORD will renew their strength. They will soar on wings like eagles; they will run and not grow weary, they will walk and not be faint.   Isaiah 40:28-31

See also: Romans 8:31, 35-39
             2 Corinthians 1:3-4
             2 Corinthians 12:9-10
             Hebrews 4:15-16
             1 Peter 3:12-14

CONTENTMENT

I am not saying this because I am in need, for I have learned to be content whatever the circumstances. I know what it is to be in need, and I know what it is to have plenty. I have learned the secret of being content in any and every situation, whether well fed or hungry, whether living in plenty or in want. I can do everything through him who gives me strength.   Philippians 4:11-13

See also: Exodus 20:17
             Hebrews 13:5

DEATH

Jesus said to her, "I am the resurrection and the life. He who believes in me will live, even though he dies; and whoever lives and believes in me will never die. Do you believe this?"   John 11:25-26

See also: John 14:1-3
             1 Corinthians 2:9
             Philippians 1:21
             Philippians 3:20

DELIVERANCE *"Because he loves me," says the LORD, "I will rescue him; I will protect him, for he acknowledges my name. He will call upon me, and I will answer him; I will be with him in trouble, I will deliver him and honor him. With long life will I satisfy him and show him my salvation."*   Psalm 91:14-16

> See also: Psalm 34
>   John 8:31-36
>   Romans 7:21-25
>   Romans 8:1-14
>   2 Corinthians 3:17

DEMONS/DEVIL *Submit yourselves, then, to God. Resist the devil, and he will flee from you.*   James 4:7

> See also: Matthew 28:18
>   Luke 10:17-20
>   Acts 5:16
>   Ephesians 6:10-18
>   1 Peter 5:8-9
>   1 John 4:1-6

DEPRESSION (SEE ANGER, ANXIETY, CONTENTMENT, FORGIVENESS, HOPE) *Cast your cares on the LORD and he will sustain you; he will never let the righteous fall.*   Psalm 55:22

> See also: Proverbs 3:5-6
>   Proverbs 18:14
>   2 Corinthians 4:8-9
>   Philippians 4:8

DIVORCE (SEE MARRIAGE) *It has been said, "Anyone who divorces his wife must give her a certificate of divorce." But I tell you that anyone who divorces his wife, except for marital unfaithfulness, causes her to become an adulteress, and anyone who marries the divorced woman commits adultery.*   Matthew 5:31-32

> See also: Matthew 19:3-9
>   1 Corinthians 7:10-15, 39

DISCOURAGEMENT (SEE ANXIETY, COMFORT, FAITH, FEAR) *"Come to me, all you who are weary and burdened, and I will give you rest. Take my yoke upon you and learn from me, for I am gentle and humble in heart, and you*

will find rest for your souls. For my yoke is easy and my burden is light."
Matthew 11:28-30

See also: Joshua 1:9
Psalm 27:14
Psalm 46:1-3
Isaiah 12:2

ENEMIES (SEE FORGIVENESS) *But I tell you: Love your enemies and pray for those who persecute you.* Matthew 5:44

See also: Proverbs 16:7
Luke 6:27-36
Romans 12:17-21
Ephesians 4:31-32
1 John 4:19-21

FAITH *Now faith is being sure of what we hope for and certain of what we do not see. . . . And without faith it is impossible to please God, because anyone who comes to him must believe that he exists and that he rewards those who earnestly seek him.* Hebrews 11:1, 6

See also: Genesis 15:6
Matthew 17:20
Mark 9:23
Mark 11:22-24
Romans 1:17
Galatians 2:20
1 Peter 1:6-9
1 John 5:4

FALSE TEACHING *Dear friends, do not believe every spirit, but test the spirits to see whether they are from God, because many false prophets have gone out into the world. This is how you can recognize the Spirit of God: Every spirit that acknowledges that Jesus Christ has come in the flesh is from God, but every spirit that does not acknowledge Jesus is not from God. This is the spirit of the antichrist, which you have heard is coming and even now is already in the world.* 1 John 4:1-3

See also: Proverbs 16:25
Colossians 2:8-10
1 Timothy 4:1-2
2 Timothy 2:15

FEAR (SEE DELIVERANCE, HOPE) *So do not fear, for I am with you; do not be dismayed, for I am your God. I will strengthen you and help you; I will uphold you with my righteous right hand.* Isaiah 41:10

See also: Psalm 27:1, 5
Psalm 91
Psalm 56:3
Isaiah 43:1-2
Romans 8:15-17
2 Timothy 1:7
Hebrews 13:6

FINANCES (SEE GIVING, CONTENTMENT) *And my God will meet all your needs according to his glorious riches in Christ Jesus.* Philippians 4:19

See also: Psalm 37:25
Malachi 3:8-10
Matthew 6:19-21, 24, 33-34
1 Timothy 6:6-10
3 John 2

FORGIVENESS (SEE ENEMIES) *Bear with each other and forgive whatever grievances you may have against one another. Forgive as the Lord forgave you.* Colossians 3:13

See also: Psalm 103:11-12
Isaiah 1:18
Isaiah 55:6-7
Matthew 6:12-15
Matthew 18:21-35
Mark 11:25
Romans 12:14-21
Ephesians 4:31-32
Hebrews 4:15-16
Hebrews 12:14-15
1 John 1:9

GIVING (SEE FINANCES) *Give, and it will be given to you. A good measure, pressed down, shaken together and running over, will be poured into your lap. For with the measure you use, it will be measured to you.* Luke 6:38

See also: Proverbs 3:9-10
Proverbs 19:17

Matthew 6:2-4
2 Corinthians 9:6-8
1 Timothy 6:17-19

GOD'S WILL *Trust in the LORD with all your heart and lean not on your own understanding; in all your ways acknowledge him, and he will make your paths straight.*   Proverbs 3:5-6
See also: Psalm 40:8
Psalm 119:97-106
Isaiah 55:8-9
James 1:5, 22

GRIEF AND BEREAVEMENT (SEE DEATH) *Jesus said to her, "I am the resurrection and the life. He who believes in me will live, even though he dies; and whoever lives and believes in me will never die. Do you believe this?"*   John 11:25-26

See also: John 14:1-3
1 Corinthians 15:12-26
2 Corinthians 5:1-6
1 Thessalonians 4:13-14
1 Peter 1:3-5
Revelation 21:4

GUILT *If we confess our sins, he is faithful and just and will forgive us our sins and purify us from all unrighteousness.*   1 John 1:9
See also: Romans 8:1
John 8:36
Isaiah 44:22

HEALING *Is any one of you in trouble? He should pray. Is anyone happy? Let him sing songs of praise. Is any one of you sick? He should call the elders of the church to pray over him and anoint him with oil in the name of the Lord. And the prayer offered in faith will make the sick person well; the Lord will raise him up. If he has sinned, he will be forgiven. Therefore confess your sins to each other and pray for each other so that you may be healed. The prayer of a righteous man is powerful and effective.*   James 5:13-16
See also: Isaiah 53:4-5
Matthew 9:35
Matthew 12:22
1 Corinthians 12:9

HOLY SPIRIT *Do not get drunk on wine, which leads to debauchery. Instead, be filled with the Spirit.*   Ephesians 5:18

      See also: Joel 2:28
                         John 14:16-17
                         Acts 1:8; 2:38
                         1 Corinthians 6:19-20
                         1 Corinthians 12:4-13
                         Ephesians 4:30

HOLY LIVING (SEE CHRISTIAN LIVING) *In the same way, count yourselves dead to sin but alive to God in Christ Jesus. Therefore do not let sin reign in your mortal body so that you obey its evil desires. Do not offer the parts of your body to sin, as instruments of wickedness, but rather offer yourselves to God, as those who have been brought from death to life; and offer the parts of your body to him as instruments of righteousness.*
                                                 Romans 6:11-13

      See also: Romans 12:1-2
                         Ephesians 4:22-24
                         James 4:8
                         1 John 2:6

HOMOSEXUALITY (SEE SEX) *Do you not know that the wicked will not inherit the kingdom of God? Do not be deceived: Neither the sexually immoral nor idolaters nor adulterers nor male prostitutes nor homosexual offenders nor thieves nor the greedy nor drunkards nor slanderers nor swindlers will inherit the kingdom of God. And that is what some of you were. But you were washed, you were sanctified, you were justified in the name of the Lord Jesus Christ and by the Spirit of our God.*
                                                1 Corinthians 6:9-11

      See also: Romans 1:16, 24-27
                         1 Timothy 1:10-11

HOPE (SEE COMFORT, FAITH) *"For I know the plans I have for you," declares the LORD, "plans to prosper you and not to harm you, plans to give you hope and a future."*   Jeremiah 29:11

      See also: Psalm 139:17-18
                         Psalm 16:11
                         Isaiah 50:7
                         Matthew 11:28-30

Philippians 1:6
Jude 24-25

JESUS CHRIST He is the image of the invisible God, the firstborn over all
creation. For by Him all things were created: things in heaven and on
earth, visible and invisible, whether thrones or powers or rulers or authori-
ties; all things were created by him and for Him. He is before all things,
and in Him all things hold together. And He is the head of the body, the
church; He is the beginning and the firstborn from among the dead, so that
in everything He might have the supremacy. For God was pleased to have
all his fullness dwell in Him, and through Him to reconcile to Himself all
things, whether things on earth or things in heaven, by making peace
through His blood, shed on the cross.   Colossians 1:15-20
    See also: John 1:1-5, 14
                Acts 4:12
                1 Corinthians 15:3-8
                1 Thessalonians 4:16-17
                1 Peter 3:18

LONELINESS (SEE CHRISTIAN FELLOWSHIP) The LORD is with me; I will not
be afraid. What can man do to me? The LORD is with me; He is my
helper. I will look in triumph on my enemies. Psalm 118:6-7
    See also: Psalm 40:1-5
                Hebrews 10:24-25

MARRIAGE (SEE DIVORCE, SEX) The LORD God said, "It is not good for
the man to be alone. I will make a helper suitable for him." . . . For this
reason a man will leave his father and mother and be united to his wife, and
they will become one flesh.   Genesis 2:18, 24
    See also: Proverbs 18:22
                Mark 10:6-9
                1 Corinthians 7:3-5
                2 Corinthians 6:14-15
                Ephesians 5:21-33
                1 Peter 3:1-7

OBEDIENCE (SEE CHRISTIANS LIVING, HOLY LIVING) We know that we have
come to know him if we obey his commands. The man who says, "I know
him," but does not do what he commands is a liar, and the truth is not in
him. But if anyone obeys his word, God's love is truly made complete in

him. *This is how we know we are in him: Whoever claims to live in him
must walk as Jesus did.*   1 John 2:3-6
    See also: Deuteronomy 11:26-28
                  1 Samuel 15:22
                  Luke 6:46
                  John 14:15, 21

PARENTING

*Children, obey your parents in the Lord, for this is right.
"Honor your father and mother" — which is the first commandment with a
promise — "that it may go well with you and that you may enjoy long life
on the earth." Fathers, do not exasperate your children; instead, bring
them up in the training and instruction of the Lord.*   Ephesians 6:1-4
    See also: Exodus 20:12
                  Deuteronomy 6:6-9
                  Proverbs 19:18; 22:6; 29:17
                  Colossians 3:20-21

PATIENCE

*Be still before the LORD and wait patiently for him; do not fret
when men succeed in their ways, when they carry out their wicked schemes.
Refrain from anger and turn from wrath; do not fret — it leads only to evil.
For evil men will be cut off, but those who hope in the LORD will inherit
the land.*   Psalm 37:7-9
    See also: Psalm 27:14
                  Psalm 40
                  Galatians 6:9
                  Philippians 1:6
                  James 5:7-11.

PEACE (SEE FAITH, HOPE)

*Let the peace of Christ rule in your hearts, since
as members of one body you were called to peace. And be thankful. Let
the word of Christ dwell in you richly as you teach and admonish one
another with all wisdom, and as you sing psalms, hymns and spiritual songs
with gratitude in your hearts to God. And whatever you do, whether in
word or deed, do it all in the name of the Lord Jesus, giving thanks to God
the Father through him.*   Colossians 3:15-17
    See also: Psalm 4:8
                  Isaiah 26:3
                  John 14:27
                  Galatians 5:22

PRAISE AND THANKSGIVING *Through Jesus, therefore, let us continually offer to God a sacrifice of praise — the fruit of lips that confess his name.*   Hebrews 13:15

See also: Psalm 34
              Psalm 92
              Psalm 103
              Habakkuk 3:17, 18
              Ephesians 3:20, 21
              Ephesians 5:20
              Philippians 4:4
              1 Thessalonians 5:16-18
              1 Peter 2:9

PRAYER *This is the confidence we have in approaching God: that if we ask anything according to his will, he hears us. And if we know that he hears us — whatever we ask — we know that we have what we asked of him.*   1 John 5:14-15

See also: Psalm 145:18-19
              Matthew 6:6-13
              Matthew 7:7-8
              John 15:7-8
              Ephesians 3:12
              Hebrews 4:14-16

PRIDE *We have different gifts, according to the grace given us. If a man's gift is prophesying, let him use it in proportion to his faith.*   Romans 12:6

See also: Proverbs 3:34
              Proverbs 16:18
              Proverbs 18:12
              James 4:6-10
              1 Peter 5:5-6

SALVATION *They replied, "Believe in the Lord Jesus, and you will be saved — you and your household."*   Acts 16:31

See also: John 3:5-7, 16-18, 36
              Romans 3:23
              Romans 5:6-11
              Romans 6:18, 22-23
              Romans 10:9-13

SEX (SEE HOMOSEXUALITY, MARRIAGE)

But among you there must not be even a hint of sexual immorality, or of any kind of impurity, or of greed, because these are improper for God's holy people.
Ephesians 5:3

See also: Leviticus 20:11-16
Psalm 119:9-11
Proverbs 5:15-23
1 Corinthians 6:12-20

SPIRITUAL GIFTS

Each one should use whatever gift he has received to serve others, faithfully administering God's grace in its various forms. If anyone speaks, he should do it as one speaking the very words of God. If anyone serves, he should do it with the strength God provides, so that in all things God may be praised through Jesus Christ. To him be the glory and the power for ever and ever. Amen.
1 Peter 4:10-11

See also: Romans 12:4-8
1 Corinthians 12:7-11
Ephesians 4:11-13

SUFFERING

Praise be to the God and Father of our Lord Jesus Christ, the Father of compassion and the God of all comfort, who comforts us in all our troubles, so that we can comfort those in any trouble with the comfort we ourselves have received from God.
2 Corinthians 1:3-4

See also: Romans 8:18, 28-29, 35, 38
James 1:2-3, 12
1 Peter 1:6-7
1 Peter 2:19-23
1 Peter 4:12-19
Revelation 21:4

TEMPTATION

No temptation has seized you except what is common to man. And God is faithful; he will not let you be tempted beyond what you can bear. But when you are tempted, he will also provide a way out so that you can stand up under it.
1 Corinthians 10:13

See also: Hebrews 2:18; 4:14-16
James 1:12-15
James 4:7-8

RECONCILIATION (SEE FORGIVENESS, SALVATION) *Therefore, if you are offering your gift at the altar and there remember that your brother has something against you, leave your gift there in front of the altar. First go and be reconciled to your brother; then come and offer your gift. Settle matters quickly with your adversary who is taking you to court. Do it while you are still with him on the way, or he may hand you over to the judge, and the judge may hand you over to the officer, and you may be thrown into prison. I tell you the truth, you will not get out until you have paid the last penny.*

Matthew 5:23-26

See also: Matthew 18:15-17
2 Corinthians 5:14-21
Colossians 1:19-20

APPENDIX E
ONE-TO-ONE MENTORING

Commitment to
SERVANT LEADERSHIP

Commitment to **MINISTRY**

Commitment to **SPIRITUAL GROWTH**

Commitment to **CHRIST**

LEADERSHIP DEVELOPMENT is a by-product of one-to-one relationships. As you disciple new and growing followers of Jesus Christ, you will identify those in whom you will want to invest more time. You may find that they desire to be equipped to minister for Christ. You may also recognize that the disciple is one who would work well with you in a mentor-protégé relationship. Each level of one-to-one mentoring fits a specific objective listed below:

COMMITMENT TO CHRIST:
We want people to receive Jesus Christ and experience forgiveness and new life in Him.

Phase One - Winning the Lost:
Friendship evangelism
Intercessory Prayer for friends and neighbors
Acts of love and deeds of kindness
Initiative events and outreach

COMMITMENT TO SPIRITUAL GROWTH:
We want Christians to become established and grow to maturity in their faith.
>   **Phase Two - Teaching a Disciple:**
>   *Steps Toward Spiritual Growth*

COMMITMENT TO MINISTRY:
We want Christians to serve God by serving others with the gifts and talents God has given them.

>   **Phase Three - Equipping for Ministry:**
>   *Steps Toward Ministry*
>   Lay Pastor Apprentice
>   Lay Pastor
>   Lay Pastor Trainer

COMMITMENT TO SERVANT LEADERSHIP:
We want to develop leaders of leaders who will impact our city and world for Christ.

>   **Phase Four - Mentoring a Protégé:**
>   Part I. Mentoring For Effective Living:
>   *Steps Toward Balancing Life's Demands*
>   Part II. Volunteer & Vocational Ministry Staff
>   Lay Pastor Leader
>   Ministry Director
>   Assistant Pastor
>   Associate Pastor or District Pastor

NOTES

LEADING A SMALL GROUP MEETING

1. These three elements of an effective small group were published by Dale E. Galloway, *20/20 Vision: How to Create a Successful Church*. (Lexington, KY: Scott Publishing Company, 1986), 111-113. Dale Galloway founded New Hope Community Church in the fall of 1972 with small groups at the heart of the ministry. Dale has taught thousands of church leaders the basic principles for effective small group ministry. For information on materials and small group or leadership seminars call 800-420-2048. Floyd Schwanz, another pastor at New Hope Community Church, presents an expanded discussion of these three elements in his book, *Growing Small Groups* (Kansas City, MO: Beacon Hill Press of Kansas City, 1995) 98-103.

SMALL GROUP DYNAMICS

1. Adapted from "Dynamic Cell Group Principles," *20/20 Vision: How to Create a Successful Church*. (Lexington, KY: Scott Publishing Company, 1986), 111-122.
2. ibid.

SHARING LEADERSHIP IN A SMALL GROUP

1. Adapted from "The Organizational Structure of the Tender Loving Care Group and How to Get a New Group Started," *20/20 Vision: How to Create a Successful Church*. (Lexington, KY: Scott Publishing Company, 1986), 147-151.
2. ibid.

MINISTRY BY PHONE

1. There may be times when it is appropriate to discuss the prayer concern. First, review the principles in the lesson, Effective Listening. Second, become familiar with the resources located in Appendix D: Ministry Contact Records. For additional help in ministry by phone consult *The Billy Graham Christian Worker's Handbook* (Minneapolis, MN: World Wide Publications. 1984) and *The Christian Counselor's Handbook* (Wheaton, IL: Tyndale House Publishing, Inc. 1987).

PRAYER MINISTRY

1. When you identify scripture that addresses the prayer concern,
    then you can pray with confidence and authority. Review the
    Selected Scriptures from Appendix D: Ministry Contact Records.
    For additional help in praying the scriptures, consult *Prayers that
    Avail Much: An Intercessor's Handbook of Scriptural Prayers*,
    Volumes 1 and 2 (Tulsa OK: Harrison House, 1989, 1991).

PROVIDING CARE

1. It is important that you are able to recall the ministry contacts
    that you have made. It is very difficult to do this by memory.
    Therefore we recommend the use of the Ministry Contact
    Records journal sheets (Appendix D). A complete copy of the
    Ministry Contact Records includes blank Ministry Contact Records
    journal pages and A to Z tabbed dividers for ring binders. It can
    be purchased separately from the publisher, Foundation of Hope,
    11731 SE Stevens Road, Portland, OR 97266, 888-248-3545 or
    503-659-5683.
2. The basic areas for helping a Christian mature in their faith are
    represented by the 12 lessons contained in the book *Steps Toward
    Spiritual Growth: One-to-one Mentoring for Spiritual Development*;
    Assurance of Salvation, Victory Over Sin and Temptation,
    Prayer, The Bible — God's Word, Sharing Your Faith, Fellowship,
    The Attributes of God, The Person of Jesus, The Holy Spirit,
    Stewardship, Obedience and Spiritual Gifts. This one-to-one dis-
    cipleship book is available in sets of two from the publisher,
    Foundation of Hope, 11731 SE Stevens Road, Portland, OR
    97266, 888-248-3545 or 503-659-5683.

INTRODUCING PEOPLE TO JESUS CHRIST

1. These two diagnostic questions are taken from the gospel
    presentation outline developed by Dr. James Kennedy at Coral
    Ridge Presbyterian Church of Fort Lauderdale, Florida. D. James
    Kennedy, *Evangelism Explosion*. 3rd ed. (Wheaton, IL: Tyndale
    House Publishers, 1996). This evangelism training program is
    one of the most successful lay witness programs in the world. For
    more information contact Evangelism Explosion, P. O. Box
    23820 Fort Lauderdale, Florida 33307 or call 954-771-8840.
2. ibid.

BIBLIOGRAPHY

The following resources are suggested reading for increased personal growth and effectiveness in ministry:

Adsit, Christopher B. *Personal Disciplemaking: A Step-by-Step Guide for Leading a Christian From New Birth to Maturity.* San Bernardino: Here's Life Publishers, 1988.

Baerg, Kevin. *Created For Excellence: 12 Keys to Godly Success.* Tacoma, WA: Inspiration Ministries, 1996.

The Billy Graham Christian Worker's Handbook. Minneapolis, MN: World Wide Publications. 1984.

Bright, Bill. *Witnessing Without Fear: How to Share Your Faith With Confidence.* San Bernardino: Here's Life Publishers, 1987.

Broom, Al and Lorraine. *One-to-one Discipling.* Vista, CA: Multiplication Ministries, 1987.

The Christian Counselor's Handbook. Wheaton, IL: Tyndale House Publishing, Inc. 1987.

Clinton, J. Robert. *The Making of a Leader.* Colorado Springs: NavPress, 1988.

Coleman, Robert E. *The Master Plan of Evangelism.* Old Tappan, NJ: Fleming H. Revell Company, 1964.

Copeland, Germaine. *A Call To Prayer: Intercession in Action.* Tulsa, OK: Harrison House, 1991.

_____. *Prayers that Avail Much: An Intercessor's Handbook of Scriptural Prayers, Vol. 1.* Tulsa, OK: Harrison House, 1989.

_____. *Prayers that Avail Much: An Intercessor's Handbook of Scriptural Prayers, Vol. 2.* Tulsa, OK: Harrison House, 1989, 1991.

Dahrens, Stephen F. *Tools for the Shepherd.* Clackamas, OR: Pastoral Support Ministries, 1988.

Durey, David D. , ed. *Ministry Skills For Small Group Leaders: 52 Training Lessons.* Portland, OR: Foundation of Hope, 1993.

Eims, Leroy. *The Lost Art of Disciple Making.* Grand Rapids, MI: Zondervan Publishing House, 1978.

Elmore, Tim. *Mentoring: How to Invest Your Life in Others.* Indianapolis, IN: Wesleyan Publishing House and Kingdom Publishing House, 1995.

_____. *The Greatest Mentors in the Bible, 32 Relationships God Used to Change the World*. Denver: Kingdom Publishing House, 1996.

Fee, Gordon. *How To Read the Bible For All Its Worth*. Grand Rapids, MI: Zondervan, 1982.

Galloway, Dale E. *The Small Group Book*. Grand Rapids, MI: Fleming H. Revell Company, 1995.

_____. *20/20 Vision: How to Create a Successful Church*. Scott Publishing Company, Lexington, KY, 1986.

Growing in Christ. Colorado Springs: NavPress, 1980.

Growing Strong in God's Family. revised ed., Colorado Springs: NavPress.

Hinckley, K.C., ed. *A Compact Guide to the Christian Life*. Colorado Springs: NavPress, 1989.

Kennedy, D. James, *Evangelism Explosion*. 4rd ed. Wheaton, IL: Tyndale House Publishers, 1996.

Lessons On Assurance. Colorado Springs: NavPress, 1980.

Little, Paul E. *How to Give Away Your Faith*. Downers Grove, IL: Inter-Varsity Press, 1966.

_____. *Know What You Believe*. Wheaton, IL: Victor Books, 1970.

Maxwell, John. *Developing The Leader Within You*. Nashville: Thomas Nelson Publishers, 1993.

_____. *Developing The Leaders Around You*. Nashville: Thomas Nelson Publishers, 1995.

McDowell, Josh, ed. *Evidence That Demands a Verdict: Historical Evidences for the Christian Faith*. San Bernardino: Here's Life Publishers, 1979.

Mears, Henrietta C. Rev. Ed. *What the Bible Is All About*. Regal Books, 1983.

Schwanz, Floyd. *Growing Small Groups*. Kansas City, MO: Beacon Hill Press of Kansas City, 1995.

Stanley, Paul D. and J. Robert Clinton. *Connecting: The Mentoring Relationships You Need to Succeed In Life*. Colorado Springs: NavPress, 1992.

RESOURCES

RESOURCES FOR SMALL GROUP MINISTRY
52 Lessons for Small Groups - Book One

52 Lessons for Small Groups - Book Two

Principles for Effective Small Group Leadership (An audio learning system for small group leaders and coaches)

Lay Pastor and Small Group Ministry Manual

RESOURCES FOR MENTORING AND EQUIPPING
Steps Toward Spiritual Growth: One-to-one Mentoring for Effective Spiritual Development

Steps Toward Ministry: One-to-one Mentoring for Effective Ministry

Steps Toward Balancing Life's Demands: One-to-one Mentoring for Effective Living

Ministry Contact Records: A Journal for Lay Pastors and Small Group Leaders

FOR ORDERS, SEMINARS OR ADDITIONAL INFORMATION:
FOUNDATION OF HOPE
11731 SE Stevens Road
Portland, OR 97266
888-248-3545
503-659-5683

ABOUT THIS BOOK

The first goal of Steps Toward Ministry is to provide a format for training and equipping Christians. There are nine lessons for effective personal ministry and three for small group leadership. These twelve modular lessons are short, simple and follow a standard format.

The apprentice begins by completing the Self-Evaluation. This helps them assess their level of competence and confidence in the 12 ministry skills. Then, using the Progress Checklist, they determine in what order they wish to complete the ministry skill lessons.

The second goal is to create an equipper, not just Christian worker. Ultimately, we want the apprentice to be empowered and encouraged to become the equipper of someone else.

Will you join us in this vision of mobilizing equippers? It starts with you inviting someone into a one-to-one equipping relationship. You can help change the world for the better, one person at a time.

ABOUT THE AUTHORS
New Hope Community Church has been a church committed to reaching the unchurched thousands by mobilizing and equipping its members to be ministers. Through the years hundreds of Lay Pastors have cared for thousands of churched and unchurched people through personal ministry and small groups.

New Hope Community Church has long been committed to raising up leaders from within. In fact, the majority of those who have served on the pastoral staff started as ministry volunteers, Lay Pastors or ministry interns. Steps Toward Ministry brings to you the insight and ministry experience of Dr. Ray Cotton and the pastoral staff of New Hope Community Church in a simple format which helps duplicate this equipping process.

There are two other mentoring books in this series: Steps Toward Spiritual Growth and Steps Toward Balancing Life's Demands. Leadership development and accelerated spiritual growth are natural by-products of one-to-one discipling, equipping and mentoring relationships. The sooner you begin, the sooner you will reap the benefits.

Resource Order Form
Foundation of Hope
11731 SE Stevens Rd.
Portland, OR 97266

Toll free (888) 248-3545   (503) 513-0282   Fax (503) 659-3993

Quantity	Resource	Price	Total
	Mentoring Tool Books		
__Packs of 2	Steps Toward Spiritual Growth	$18/pack	$
__Packs of 2	Steps Toward Ministry	$18/pack	$
__Packs of 2	Steps Toward Balancing Life's Demands	$18/pack	$
__Packs of 6	Special Mentoring Package 2 each of the above 3 books	$50/pack	$
	Bible Study Lessons		
__Each	52 Lessons for Small Groups - Book One	$20 each	$
__Each	52 Lessons for Small Groups - Book Two	$20 each	$
Shipping and Handling Costs. Add 10% *($5.00 minimum)*			$
TOTAL AMOUNT DUE *(U.S. Funds only)*			$

Name: _____ Day ph# ( ) _____ Eve ph# ( )

Church: _____ Church ph# ( )

Address (Church or Home - circle one): _____

City: _____ State: _____ Zip:

Method of payment (circle one):   Bill   Check   Cash: $ MC/VISA

Charge card #: _____ - _____ - _____   Exp. Date: /

❏ I am interested in the October, 1998 Church Growth Conference.

❏ I am interested in having a seminar on Small Groups/Mentoring at my church.

❏ I am interested in the "Becoming Soul Mates" seminar with Drs. Les and Leslie Parrot.